Also by Twyla Tharp

Push Comes to Shove: An Autobiography

TWYLA THARP
THE CREATIVE HABIT
LEARN IT AND USE IT FOR LIFE

A PRACTICAL GUIDE

WITH MARK REITER

SIMON & SCHUSTER
New York   London   Toronto   Sydney   Singapore

SIMON & SCHUSTER
Rockefeller Center
1230 Avenue of the Americas
New York, NY 10020

SIMON & SCHUSTER and colophon are registered trademarks
of Simon & Schuster, Inc.

For information about special discounts for bulk purchases,
please contact Simon & Schuster Special Sales:
1-800-456-6798 or business@simonandschuster.com.

Designed by Julian Peploe

Manufactured in the United States of America

1   3   5   7   9   10   8   6   4   2

Library of Congress Cataloging-in-Publication Data
Tharp, Twyla.
The creative habit : learn it and use it for life : a practical
guide / Twyla Tharp, with Mark Reiter.
p. cm.
1. Creative ability. 2. Creative thinking. 3. Creation (Literary, artistic, etc.).
I. Reiter, Mark. II. Title.
BF408.T415 2003
153.3'5—dc22   2003057389

ISBN 0-7432-3526-6

The authors and publisher gratefully acknowledge permission to reprint the following materials:

p. 18: "Two Sketches of Beethoven by J. D. Böhm, between 1820 and 1825" (courtesy of Beethoven-haus, Bonn), from Oscar G. Sonneck, ed., *Beethoven: Impressions by His Contemporaries* (Dover Publications, 1926).

p.153: Buster Keaton, *Steamboat Bill, Jr.* (United Artists, 1928), 3 stills; courtesy of the Academy of Motion Picture Arts and Sciences.

p. 172: Two sketches of waves, from *The Notebooks of Leonardo da Vinci,* compiled and edited from the original manuscripts by Jean Paul Richter (Dover Publications [1970]).

p. 241: *(Left)* Rembrandt, *Artist in His Studio,* c. 1627–28; photograph © 2003 Museum of Fine Arts, Boston. *(Right)* Rembrandt, *Self Portrait with Two Circles,* c. 1665; courtesy of the English Heritage Photographic Library/Kenwood House.

To my mother, Lecille Confer Tharp,
for making sure I had all the tools I would need.

To my father, William Albert Tharp,
for giving me the DNA to build things from scratch.

To my son, Jesse Alexander Huot,
for helping me create each new day.

And those who had seen it told how he who had
been possessed with demons was healed.

—Luke 8:36

CONTENTS

The Creative Habit

Chapter 1

I walk into a

white room

I walk into a large white room. It's a dance studio in midtown Manhattan. I'm wearing a sweatshirt, faded jeans, and Nike cross-trainers. The room is lined with eight-foot-high mirrors. There's a boom box in the corner. The floor is clean, virtually spotless if you don't count the thousands of skid marks and footprints left there by dancers rehearsing. Other than the mirrors, the boom box, the skid marks, and me, the room is empty.

In five weeks I'm flying to Los Angeles with a troupe of six dancers to perform a dance program for eight consecutive evenings in front of twelve hundred people every night. It's my troupe. I'm the choreographer. I have half of the program in hand—a fifty-minute ballet for all six dancers set to Beethoven's twenty-

4

ninth piano sonata, the "Hammerklavier." I created the piece more than a year ago on many of these same dancers, and I've spent the past few weeks rehearsing it with the company.

The other half of the program is a mystery. I don't know what music I'll be using. I don't know which dancers I'll be working with. I have no idea what the costumes will look like, or the lighting, or who will be performing the music. I have no idea of the length of the piece, although it has to be long enough to fill the second half of a full program to give the paying audience its money's worth.

The length of the piece will dictate how much rehearsal time I need. This, in turn, means getting on the phone to dancers, scheduling studio time, and getting the ball rolling—all on the premise that something wonderful will come out of what I fashion in the next few weeks in this empty white room.

My dancers expect me to deliver because my choreography represents their livelihood. The presenters in Los Angeles expect the same because they've sold a lot of tickets to people with the promise that they'll see something new and interesting from me. The theater owner (without really thinking about it) expects it as well; if I don't show up, his theater will be empty for a week. That's a lot of people, many of whom I've never met, counting on me to be creative.

But right now I'm not thinking about any of this. I'm in a room with the obligation to create a major dance piece. The dancers will be here in a few minutes. What are we going to do?

To some people, this empty room symbolizes something profound, mysterious, and terrifying: the task of starting with nothing and working your way toward creating something whole and beautiful and satisfying. It's no different for a writer rolling a fresh sheet of paper into his typewriter (or more likely firing up the blank screen on his computer), or a painter confronting a virginal canvas, a sculptor staring at a raw chunk of stone, a composer at the piano with his fingers hovering just above the keys. Some people find this moment—the moment before creativity begins—so painful that they simply cannot deal with it. They get up and walk away from the computer, the canvas, the keyboard; they take a nap or go shopping or fix lunch or do chores around the house. They procrastinate. In its most extreme form, this terror totally paralyzes people.

The blank space can be humbling. But I've faced it my whole professional life. It's my job. It's also my calling. Bottom line: Filling this empty space constitutes my identity.

I'm a dancer and choreographer. Over the last 35 years, I've created 130 dances and ballets. Some of them are good, some less good (that's an understatement—some were public humiliations). I've worked with dancers in almost every space and environment you can imagine. I've rehearsed in cow pastures. I've rehearsed in hundreds of studios, some luxurious in their austerity and expansiveness, others filthy and gritty, with rodents literally racing around the edges of the room. I've spent eight months on a film set in Prague, choreographing the dances and directing the opera sequences for Milos Forman's *Amadeus*. I've staged sequences for horses in New York City's Central Park for the film *Hair*. I've worked with dancers in the opera houses of London, Paris, Stockholm, Sydney, and Berlin. I've run my own company for three decades. I've created and directed a hit show on Broadway. I've worked long enough and produced with sufficient consistency that by now I find not only challenge and trepidation but peace as well as promise in the empty white room. It has become my home.

After so many years, I've learned that being creative is a full-time job with its own daily patterns. That's why writers, for example, like to establish routines for themselves. The most productive ones get started early in the morning, when the world is quiet, the phones aren't ringing, and their minds are rested, alert, and not yet polluted by other people's words. They might set a goal for themselves—write fifteen hundred words, or stay at their desk until noon—but the real secret is that they do this every day. In other words, they are disciplined. Over time, as the daily routines become second nature, discipline morphs into habit.

It's the same for any creative individual, whether it's a painter finding his way each morning to the easel, or a medical researcher returning daily to the laboratory. The routine is as much a part of the creative process as the lightning bolt of inspiration, maybe more. And this routine is available to everyone.

Creativity is not just for artists. It's for businesspeople looking for a new way to close a sale; it's for engineers trying to solve a problem; it's for parents who want their children to see the world in more than one way. Over the past four decades, I have been engaged in one creative pursuit or another every day, in both my professional and my personal life. I've thought a great deal about what it means to be creative, and how to go about it efficiently. I've also learned from the painful experience of going about it in the worst possible way. I'll tell you about both. And I'll give you exercises that will challenge some of your creative assumptions—to make you stretch, get stronger, last longer. After all, you stretch before you jog, you loosen up before you work out, you practice before you play. It's no different for your mind.

I will keep stressing the point about creativity being augmented by routine and habit. Get used to it. In these pages a philosophical tug of war will periodically rear its head. It is the perennial debate, born in the Romantic era, between the beliefs that all creative acts are born of (a) some transcendent, inexplicable Dionysian act of inspiration, a kiss from God on your brow that allows you to give the world *The Magic Flute,* or (b) hard work.

If it isn't obvious already, I come down on the side of hard work. That's why this book is called *The Creative Habit.* Creativity is a habit, and the best creativity is a result of good work habits. That's it in a nutshell.

The film *Amadeus* (and the play by Peter Shaffer on which it's based) dramatizes and romanticizes the divine origins of creative genius. Antonio Salieri, representing the talented hack, is cursed to live in the time of Mozart, the gifted and undisciplined genius who writes as though touched by the hand of God. Salieri recognizes the depth of Mozart's genius, and is tortured that God has chosen someone so unworthy to be His divine creative vessel.

Of course, this is hogwash. There are no "natural" geniuses. Mozart was his father's son. Leopold Mozart had gone through an arduous education, not just in music, but also in philosophy and religion; he was a sophisticated, broad-thinking man, famous throughout Europe as a composer and pedagogue. This is not news to music lovers. Leopold had a massive influence on his young son. I question how much of a "natural" this young boy was. Genetically, of course, he was probably more inclined to write music than, say, play basketball, since he was only three feet tall when he captured the public's attention. But his first good fortune was to have a father who was a composer and a virtuoso on the violin, who could approach keyboard instruments with skill, and who upon recognizing some ability in his son, said to himself, "This is interesting. He likes music. Let's see how far we can take this."

Leopold taught the young Wolfgang everything about music, including counterpoint and harmony. He saw to it that the boy was exposed to everyone in Europe who was writing good music or could be of use in Wolfgang's musical development. Destiny, quite often, is a determined parent. Mozart was hardly some naive prodigy who sat down at the keyboard and, with God whispering in his ears, let the music flow from his fingertips. It's a nice image for selling tickets to movies, but whether or not God has kissed your brow, you still have to work. Without learning and preparation, you won't know how to harness the power of that kiss.

Nobody worked harder than Mozart. By the time he was twenty-eight years old, his hands were deformed because of all the hours he had spent practicing, performing, and gripping a quill pen to compose. That's the missing element in the popular portrait of Mozart. Certainly, he had a gift that set him apart from others. He was the most complete musician imaginable, one who wrote for all instruments in all combinations, and no one has written greater music for the human voice. Still, few people, even those hugely gifted, are capable of the application and focus that Mozart displayed throughout his short life. As Mozart himself wrote to a friend, "People err who think my art comes easily to me. I assure you, dear friend, nobody has devoted so much time and thought to composition as I. There is not a famous master whose music I have not industriously studied through many times." Mozart's focus was fierce; it had to be for him to deliver the music he did in his relatively short life, under the conditions he endured, writing in coaches and delivering scores just before the curtain went up, dealing with the distractions of raising a family and the constant need for money. Whatever scope and grandeur you attach to Mozart's musical gift, his so-called genius, his discipline and work ethic were its equal.

I'm sure this is what Leopold Mozart saw so early in his son who, as a three-year-old, one day impulsively jumped up on the stool to play his older sister's harpsichord—and was immediately smitten. Music quickly became Mozart's passion, his preferred activity. I seriously doubt that Leopold had to tell his son for very long, "Get in there and practice your music." The child did it on his own.

More than anything, this book is about preparation: In order to be creative you have to know how to prepare to be creative.

No one can give you your subject matter, your creative content; if they could, it would be their creation and not yours. But there's a process that generates creativity—and you can learn it. And you can make it habitual.

There's a paradox in the notion that creativity should be a habit. We think of creativity as a way of keeping everything fresh and new, while habit implies routine and repetition. That paradox intrigues me because it occupies the place where creativity and skill rub up against each other.

It takes skill to bring something you've imagined into the world: to use words to create believable lives, to select the colors and textures of paint to represent a haystack at sunset, to combine ingredients to make a flavorful dish. No one is born with that skill. It is developed through exercise, through repetition, through a blend of learning and reflection that's both painstaking and rewarding. And it takes time. Even Mozart, with all his innate gifts, his passion for music, and his father's devoted tutelage, needed to get twenty-four youthful symphonies under his belt before he composed something enduring with number twenty-five. If art is the bridge between what you see in your mind and what the world sees, then skill is how you build that bridge.

That's the reason for the exercises. They will help you develop skill. Some might seem simple. Do them anyway—you can never spend enough time on the basics. Before he could write *Così fan tutte,* Mozart had practiced his scales.

While modern dance and ballet are my métier, they are not the subject of this book. I promise you that the text will not be littered with dance jargon. You will not be confused by first positions and pliés and tendus in these pages. I will assume that you're a reasonably sophisticated and open-minded person. I hope you've been to the ballet and seen a dance company in action on stage. If you haven't, shame on you; that's like admitting you've never read a novel or strolled through a museum or heard a Beethoven symphony live. If you give me that much, we can work together.

The way I figure it, my work habits are applicable to everyone. You'll find that I'm a stickler about preparation. My daily routines are transactional. Everything that happens in my day is a transaction between the external world and my internal world. Everything is raw material. Everything is relevant. Everything is usable. Everything feeds into my creativity. But without proper preparation, I cannot see it, retain it, and use it. Without the time and effort invested in getting ready to create, you can be hit by the thunderbolt and it'll just leave you stunned.

Take, for example, a wonderful scene in the film *The Karate Kid.* The teenaged Daniel asks the wise and wily Mr. Miyagi to teach him karate. The old man agrees and orders Daniel first to wax his car in precisely opposed circular motions ("Wax on, wax off"). Then he tells Daniel to paint his wooden fence in precise up and down motions. Finally, he makes Daniel hammer nails to repair a wall. Daniel is puzzled at first, then angry. He wants to learn the martial arts so he can defend himself. Instead he is confined to household chores. When Daniel is finished restoring Miyagi's car, fence, and walls, he explodes with rage at his "mentor." Miyagi physically attacks Daniel, who without thought or hesitation defends himself with the core thrusts and parries of karate. Through Miyagi's deceptively simple chores, Daniel has absorbed the basics of karate—without knowing it.

In the same spirit as Miyagi teaches karate, I hope this book will help you be more creative. I can't guarantee that everything you'll create will be wonderful—that's up to you—but I do promise that if you read through the book and heed even half the suggestions, you'll never be afraid of a blank page or an empty canvas or a white room again. Creativity will become your habit.

Chapter 2

rituals

of preparation

I begin each day of my life with a ritual: I wake up at 5:30 A.M., put on my workout clothes, my leg warmers, my sweatshirts, and my hat. I walk outside my Manhattan home, hail a taxi, and tell the driver to take me to the Pumping Iron gym at 91st Street and First Avenue, where I work out for two hours. The ritual is not the stretching and weight training I put my body through each morning at the gym; the ritual is the cab. The moment I tell the driver where to go I have completed the ritual.

It's a simple act, but doing it the same way each morning habitualizes it—makes it repeatable, easy to do. It reduces the chance that I would skip it or do it differently. It is one more item in my arsenal of routines, and one less thing to think about.

Some people might say that simply stumbling out of bed and getting into a taxicab hardly rates the honorific "ritual." It glorifies a mundane act that anyone can perform.

I disagree. First steps are hard; it's no one's idea of fun to wake up in the dark every day and haul one's tired body to the gym. Like everyone, I have days when I wake up, stare at the ceiling, and ask myself, Gee, do I feel like working out today? But the quasi-religious power I attach to this ritual keeps me from rolling over and going back to sleep.

It's vital to establish some rituals—automatic but decisive patterns of behavior—at the beginning of the creative process, when you are most at peril of turning back, chickening out, giving up, or going the wrong way.

A ritual, the *Oxford English Dictionary* tells me, is "a prescribed order of performing religious or other devotional service." All that applies to my morning ritual. Thinking of it as a ritual has a transforming effect on the activity.

Turning something into a ritual eliminates the question, Why am I doing this? By the time I give the taxi driver directions, it's too late to wonder why I'm going to the gym and not snoozing under the warm covers of my bed. The cab is moving. I'm committed. Like it or not, I'm going to the gym.

The ritual erases the question of whether or not I like it. It's also a friendly reminder that I'm doing the right thing. (I've done it before. It was good. I'll do it again.)

We all have rituals in our day, whether we're aware of them or not.

A friend, a hard-boiled pragmatist with not a spiritual bone in his body, practices yoga in the morning in his home to overcome back pain. He starts each session by lighting a candle. He doesn't need the candle to do his poses (although the mild glow and the faint scent have a tonic effect, he says), but the ceremonial act of lighting this votive candle transforms yoga into a sanctifying ritual. It means he's taking the session seriously, and that for the next ninety minutes he is committed to practicing yoga. Candle. Click. Yoga. An automatic three-step call-and-response mechanism that anchors his morning. When he's done, he blows out the candle and goes on with the rest of his day.

An executive I know begins each day with a twenty-minute meeting with her assistant. It's a simple organizational tool, but turning it into a daily ceremony for two people intensifies the bond between them and gives their day a predictable, repeatable kick-start. They don't have to think about what to do when they arrive at the office. They already know it's their twenty-minute ritual.

Dancers are totally governed by ritual. It begins with class from 10:00 A.M. to noon every day, where they stretch and warm up their muscles and put their bodies through the classic dance positions. They do this daily, without fail, because all dancers working in class know that their efforts at strengthening the muscles will armor them against injury in rehearsal or performance. What makes it a ritual is that they do it without questioning the need.

As with all sacred rites, the beginning of class is beautiful to watch. The dancers may straggle in and mill about, but they eventually assume, with frighteningly formal rigor, their customary place at the barre or on the floor. If a principal dancer walks in, they automatically shift places to give the star the center spot facing the mirror. Of such beliefs and traditions are rituals made. It's like going to church. We rarely question why we go to church, and we don't expect concrete answers when we do. We just know it feeds our spirit somehow, and so we do it.

A lot of habitually creative people have preparation rituals linked to the setting in which they choose to start their day. By putting themselves into that environment, they begin their creative day.

The composer Igor Stravinsky did the same thing every morning when he entered his studio to work: He sat at the piano and played a Bach fugue. Perhaps he needed the ritual to feel like a musician, or the playing somehow connected him to musical notes, his vocabulary. Perhaps he was honoring his hero, Bach, and seeking his blessing for the day. Perhaps it was nothing more than a simple method to get his fingers moving, his motor running, his mind thinking music. But repeating the routine each day in the studio induced some click that got him started.

I know a chef who begins each day in the meticulously tended urban garden that dominates the tiny terrace of his Brooklyn home. He is obsessed with fresh ingredients, particularly herbs, spices, and flowers. Spending the first minutes of the day among his plants is his ideal creative environment for thinking about new flavor combinations and dishes. He putters about, feeling connected to nature, and this gets him going. Once he picks a vegetable or herb, he can't let it sit there. He has to head off to the restaurant and start cooking.

A painter I know can't do anything in her studio without propulsive music pounding out of the speakers. Turning it on turns on a switch inside her. The beat gets her into a groove. It's the metronome for her creative life.

A writer friend can only write outside. He can't stand the thought of being chained indoors to his word processor while a "great day" is unfolding outside. He fears he's missing something stirring in the air. So he lives in Southern California and carries his coffee mug out to work in the warmth of an open porch in his backyard. Mystically, he now believes he is missing nothing.

In the end, there is no one ideal condition for creativity. What works for one person is useless for another. The only criterion is this: Make it easy on yourself. Find a working environment where the prospect of wrestling with your muse doesn't scare you, doesn't shut you down. It should make you want to be there, and once you find it, stick with it. To get the creative habit, you need a working environment that's habit-forming.

All preferred working states, no matter how eccentric, have one thing in common: When you enter into them, they impel you to get started. Whether it's the act of carrying a hot coffee mug to an outdoor porch, or the rock 'n' roll that gets a painter revved up to splash color on a canvas, or the stillness of an herb garden that puts a chef in a culinary trance, moving inside each of these routines gives you no choice but to *do something*. It's Pavlovian: follow the routine, get a creative payoff.

Athletes know the power of a triggering ritual. A pro golfer may walk along the fairway chatting with his caddie, his playing partner, a friendly official or scorekeeper, but when he stands behind the ball and takes a deep breath, he has signaled to himself that it's time to concentrate. A basketball player comes to the free-throw line, touches his socks, his shorts, receives the ball, bounces it exactly three times, and then he is ready to rise and shoot, exactly as he's done a hundred times a day in practice. By making the start of the sequence automatic, they replace doubt and fear with comfort and routine.

It worked for Beethoven, too, as these sketches, rendered between 1820 and 1825 by J. D. Böhm, show. Although he was not physically fit, Beethoven would

start each day with the same ritual: a morning walk during which he would scribble into a pocket sketchbook the first rough notes of whatever musical idea inevitably entered his head. Having done that, having limbered up his mind and transported himself into his version of a trance zone during the walk, he would return to his room and get to work.

As for me, my preferred working state is thermal—I need heat—and my preferred ritual is getting warm. That's why I start my day at the gym. I am in perpetual pursuit of body warmth. It can never be too hot for me. Even in the middle of sweltering August, when the rest of New York is half frozen in the comforts of air-conditioning, I have all the windows and doors of my apartment wide open as if to say, "Hello, heat!" I loathe air-conditioning. I like skin that is just about to break out in glistening sweat.

There's also a psychological component to heat: It calls up the warmth of the hearth and home. In a word, it says "mother," which is all about feeling safe and secure. A warm, secure dancer can work without fear. In that state of physical and psychic warmth, dancers touch their moments of greatest physical potential. They're not afraid to try new movements. They can trust their bodies, and that's when magic happens. When they're not warm, dancers are afraid—afraid of injury, afraid of looking bad to others, afraid they're falling short of the inner bar they set for themselves. That's a rotten state to be in.

There's a practical reason for this, of course. Unlike other art forms, dance is all about physical movement and exertion. Even in my sixties, I need to keep my muscles in a state of readiness to pursue my craft, so that when I demonstrate a step in rehearsal I can actually execute it with some amplitude and grace and not hurt myself. Every athlete knows this: warm up before playing or you'll pull a muscle. If I am warm, I feel I can do anything.

My morning workout ritual is the most basic form of self-reliance; it reminds me that, when all else fails, I can at least depend on myself. It's my algebra of self-reliance: I depend on my body in order to work, and I am more productive if my body is strong. My daily workout is a part of my preparation for work.

This, more than anything else, is what rituals of preparation give us: They arm us with confidence and self-reliance. The talent agent Sam Cohn tells a story about an entertainment lawyer named Burton Meyer who taught him a great lesson through a daily ritual. Cohn was working at CBS at the time, and Meyer thought he was working too hard for CBS and not enjoying himself enough. "You're overcommitted," he told Cohn. "You know, I practice law for fun. I don't have to do this. And I'll tell you how that came about. Ever since I was a young lawyer, each day I would come back from lunch and I would close my office door, I would sit in my chair, and for one hour I would quietly ruminate on one question. And the question was this: Burt, what's in it for you?"

A ritual of asking "What's in it for me?" might not provide the most open-minded philosophy of life, but it will keep you focused on your goals. Taken to extremes, it's an unattractive way of seeing the world, but it does place your motivation right smack in front of you.

When I walk into the white room I am alone, but I am alone with my:

body ambition
needs memories
distractions fears

ideas passions
goals prejudices

These ten items are at the heart of who I am. Whatever I'm going to create will be a reflection of how these have shaped my life, and how I've learned to channel my experiences into them.

The last two—distractions and fears—are the dangerous ones. They're the habitual demons that invade the launch of every project. No one starts a creative endeavor without a certain amount of fear; the key is to learn how to keep free-floating fears from paralyzing you before you've begun. When I feel that sense of dread, I try to make it as specific as possible. Let me tell you my five big fears:

1. People will laugh at me.
2. Someone has done it before.
3. I have nothing to say.
4. I will upset someone I love.
5. Once executed, the idea will never be as good as it is in my mind.

These are mighty demons, but they're hardly unique to me. You probably share some. If I let them, they'll shut down my impulses ("No, you can't do that") and perhaps turn off the spigots of creativity altogether. So I combat my fears with a staring-down ritual, like a boxer looking his opponent right in the eye before a bout.

1. People will laugh at me? Not the people I respect; they haven't yet, and they're not going to start now. (Some others have. London's *Evening Standard* from 1966: "Three girls, one of them named Twyla Tharp, appeared at the Albert Hall last evening and threatened to do the same tonight." So what? Thirty-seven years later I'm still here.)

2. Someone has done it before? Honey, it's *all* been done before. Nothing's really original. Not Homer or Shakespeare and certainly not you. Get over yourself.

3. I have nothing to say? An irrelevant fear. We all have something to say. Plus, you're panicking too soon. If the dancers don't walk out on you, chances are the audience won't either.

4. I will upset someone I love? A serious worry that is not easily exorcised or stared down because you never know how loved ones will respond to your creation. The best you can do is remind yourself that you're a good person with good intentions. You're trying to create unity, not discord. See the curtain call. See the people standing up. Hear the crowd roaring.

5. Once executed, the idea will never be as good as it is in my mind? Toughen up. Leon Battista Alberti, a fifteenth-century architectural theorist, said, "Errors accumulate in the sketch and compound in the model." But better an imperfect dome in Florence than cathedrals in the clouds.

In those long and sleepless nights when I'm unable to shake my fears sufficiently, I borrow a biblical epigraph from Dostoyevsky's *The Demons:* I see my fears being cast into the bodies of wild boars and hogs, and I watch them rush to a cliff where they fall to their deaths.

It's a little more extreme than counting sheep, but it's far more effective for me.

This is a head game, of course. What ritual isn't? Maybe it's a little pathetic that after all this time I need this sort of pep talk to deal with my demons, but the unknown is a fearful place, and anything new is a step into the unknown. That fear is why ancient cultures created rituals in the first place. They lived in constant fear of other tribes, of predatory animals, of nature and the weather, all of which they believed were controlled by one or many awesome and awful deities. They hoped to gain control over their food supply, their herds, their fertility, their safety—their fears—by appeasing the gods with rituals. They would kill a certain kind of animal, and bleed it in a special way, and stack it on a fire, and toss some more animals into the flame, and offer the blood in a gold flask to the heavens—because doing so would guarantee a healthy crop or victory in battle. Rituals seduced the primitive tribes into believing they could control the uncontrollable.

Centuries later, the ancient rituals seem silly (unless, of course, you believe in them). But are they that much different from all the rituals, big and small, that we employ to get through the day? I remember being a very ritualistic kid. I think most kids are. Eager to gain some control over their lives, they concoct games and rites to add sense and form to their world. The dolls have to sit a certain way on the bed. The socks go on their feet before the pants. The walk to school has to be on the north side of the street; the walk back home has to retrace the steps perfectly. When I said my prayers as a child, I was convinced that I had to say so many words during the exhale and so many words on the inhale, or something bad would happen. Weird, right? Not really. Though less brutal, it's not that far removed from slaughtering a cow and offering it to an unseen god to ensure rain.

I know a writer who looks for something to clean around the house when the words aren't coming out. As he sits in front of his computer, feeling stale and stalled, everything around him looks grimy and caked with dust. So he grabs a rag and a spray bottle of Fantastik and gets to work on the crud. When everything is clean and shiny, he sits back down at the screen and the words invariably flow.

He has a sophisticated explanation for why this ritual works, involving neural pathways and emotions and identity and self-worth. The job of a writer, he says, is simple: You write what's in your head. But it becomes an emotional challenge when you can't corral the words into coherent thoughts. Suddenly you doubt yourself. As you wallow in self-doubt, you turn away from the computer screen and see dirt that you hadn't noticed before (certainly not when the work was going well and you didn't need to turn away from the screen); the dirt becomes inextricably linked with the self-doubt, and wiping away the grime cathartically wipes away the self-doubt. The emotional crisis is solved. Let the writing begin.

Personally, I think the key to his cleaning ritual is the fact that he gets up and moves. Movement stimulates our brains in ways we don't appreciate. But I give some credence to his cute metaphorical link between dirt and doubt. It might be mumbo jumbo, but mystery and mumbo jumbo are a big part of ritual, too. And if it works, why question it.

I know a businessman who has a ritual of unfolding a dollar bill at the start of each deal and staring at it in silence for a moment, because there on the bill, opposite the Great Seal with the bald eagle and the overly ripe E Pluribus Unum, above the mysteriously cropped pyramid with the floating eye, is the motto *Annuit coeptis:* "Providence has favored our undertakings." To some, this might seem superstitious, but a superstition is nothing more than a ritual repeated religiously. The habit, and the faith invested in it, converts it into an act that provides comfort and strength. Every business deal is an act of courage and faith to this executive, and the motto on the dollar bill is his blessing.

The mechanism by which we convert the chemistry of pessimism into optimism is still uncharted. But we do know how debilitating negativity can be and, likewise, how productive optimism is. I am no stranger to pessimism and fear. They can descend on me at night, during those 3:00 A.M. sessions when I can't sleep and I'm consumed by my litany of "issues." My mind flits from the major issues of how to cope with everything I want to do, to the minor housekeeping details of going to a manicurist to repair my splitting fingernails. At times like this, priorities go astray; a trifle, such as my nails, can leap into the foreground of my fears. I swoon deeper and deeper into a fog of self-doubt and confusion. But rituals help me clear the fog.

The other obstacle to good work, as harmful as one's fears, is distractions.

I know there are people who can assimilate a lot of incoming data from all angles—from newspapers and magazines, movies, television, music, friends, the Internet—and turn it into something wonderful. They thrive on a multitude of stimuli, the more complicated the better. I'm not hard-wired that way. When I

25

commit to a project, I don't expand my contact with the world; I try to cut it off. I want to place myself in a bubble of monomaniacal absorption where I'm fully invested in the task at hand.

As a result, I find I'm often subtracting things from my life rather than adding them. I've turned that into a ritual as well. I list the biggest distractions in my life and make a pact with myself to do without them for a week. Here are some perennially tempting distractions that I cut out:

Movies:
This is painful, because I love films and cutting them out costs me something. My parents owned a drive-in movie theater in San Bernardino, California, and I spent a huge part of my childhood working there watching movies. But when I'm absorbed by a project, unless I'm looking at a film to learn something specific, I don't go to movie theaters and I don't rent videos. If I started watching movies for pleasure, I'd become addicted. I'd watch all day and never get anything done.

Multitasking:
In an accelerated, overachieving world, we all take pride in our ability to do two or more things at the same time: working on vacation; using an elegant dinner to hammer out a business deal; reading while we're groaning on the StairMaster. The irony of multitasking is that it's exhausting; when you're doing two or three things simultaneously, you use more energy than the sum of energy required to do each task independently. You're also cheating yourself because you're not doing anything excellently. You're compromising your virtuosity. In the words of T. S. Eliot, you're "distracted from distractions by distractions."

It's a challenge to cut out multitasking because we all get a frisson of satisfaction from being able to keep several balls in the air at once. But one week without multitasking is worth it; the increased focus and awareness are their own rewards.

Numbers: More than anything, I can live without numbers—the ones on clocks, dials, meters, bathroom scales, bills, contracts, tax forms, bank statements, and royalty reports. For one week I tell myself to "stop counting." I don't look at anything with a number in it. This is not that great a hardship; it means mostly that I don't have to deal with grinding business details. The goal is to give the left side of the brain—the hemisphere that does the counting—a rest and let the more intuitive right hemisphere come to the fore.

Background Music: I know there are artists who like music in the background when they work; they use the music to block out everything else. They're not listening to it; it's there as a form of companionship. I don't need a soundtrack to accompany my life. Music in the background nibbles away at your awareness. It's comforting, perhaps, but who said tapping into your awareness was supposed to be comfortable? And who knows how much of your brainpower and intuition the Muzak is draining? When I listen to music, I don't multitask; I simply listen. Part of it is my job: I listen to music to see if I can dance to it. But another part is simple courtesy to the composer. I listen with the same intensity the composer exerted to string the notes together. I'd expect the same from anyone watching my work. I certainly wouldn't approve if someone read a book while my dancers were performing.

I don't recommend living without distractions as a permanent lifestyle for anyone. It's too monastic. But anyone can do it for a week, and the payoff will surprise you.

It's a simple equation: Subtracting your dependence on some of the things you take for granted increases your independence. It's liberating, forcing you to rely on your own ability rather than your customary crutches.

There's an American tradition of giving things up to foster self-reliance. Ralph Waldo Emerson was a man of the world who sought solitude and simplicity. Henry David Thoreau turned his back on the distractions of life in society in pursuit of a better and clearer life, and found a rich vein of inspiration and invention in the Massachusetts woods. Emily Dickinson lived as quiet and constricted a life as one can imagine, and channeled her energies directly into her poetry. All three sought lives apart from the hubbub of the city's commerce—and they didn't even have to cope with the roar of the car, the drone of the radio, the blur of television, or the information surfeit of the Internet.

The act of giving something up does not merely clear time and mental space to focus you. It's a ritual, too, an offering where you sacrifice a portion of your life to the metaphoric gods of creation. Instead of goats or cattle, we're sacrificing television or music or numbers—and what is a sacrifice but a ritual?

When you have selected the environment that works for you, developed the start-up ritual that impels you forward every day, faced down your fears, and put your distractions in their proper place, you have cleared the first hurdle. You have begun to prepare to begin.

exercises

1 Where's Your "Pencil"?

In his lovely essay "Why Write?," the novelist Paul Auster tells a story about growing up as an eight-year-old in New York City and being obsessed with baseball, particularly the New York Giants. The only thing he remembers about attending his first major league baseball game at the Polo Grounds with his parents and friends is that he saw his idol, Willie Mays, outside the players' locker room after the game. The young Auster screwed up his courage and approached the great centerfielder. "Mr. Mays," he said, "could I please have your autograph?"

"Sure, kid, sure," the obliging Mays replied. "You got a pencil?"

Auster didn't have a pencil on him, neither did his father or his mother or anyone else in his group.

Mays waited patiently, but when it became obvious that no one present had anything to write with, he shrugged and said, "Sorry, kid. Ain't got no pencil, can't give no autograph."

From that day on, Auster made it a habit to never leave the house without a pencil in his pocket. "It's not that I had any particular plans for that pencil," Auster writes, "but I didn't want to be unprepared. I had been caught empty-handed once, and I wasn't about to let it happen again. If nothing else, the years have taught me this: If there's a pencil in your pocket, there's a good chance that one day you'll feel tempted to start using it. As I like to tell my children, that's how I became a writer."

What is your pencil? What is the one tool that feeds your creativity and is so essential that without it you feel naked and unprepared?

A Manhattan writer I know never leaves his apartment without reminding himself to "come back with a face." Whether he's walking down the street or sitting on a park bench or riding the subway or standing on a checkout line, he looks for a compelling face and works up a rich description of it in his mind. When he has a moment, he writes it all down in his notebook. Not only does the exercise warm up his descriptive powers, but studying the crags, lines, and bumps of a stranger's face forces him to imagine that individual's life. Sometimes, if he's lucky, the writer attaches a complete biography to the face, and then a name, and then a narrative. Before he knows it, he has the ingredients for a full-fledged story.

I know cartoonists who always carry pen and pad to sketch what they see, photographers who always have a camera in their pockets, composers who carry Dictaphones to capture a snatch of vagabond melody that pops into their heads. They are always prepared.

Pick your "pencil" and don't leave home without it.

2 Build Up Your Tolerance for Solitude

Some people are autophobic. They're afraid to be alone. The thought of going into a room to work all by themselves pains them in a way that is, at first, paralyzing within the room, and then keeps them from entering the room altogether.

It's not the solitude that slays a creative person. It's all that solitude *without a purpose*. You're alone, you're suffering, and you don't have a good reason for putting yourself through that misery. To build up your tolerance for solitude, you need a goal.

Sit alone in a room and let your thoughts go wherever they will. Do this for one minute. (Anyone can handle one minute of daydreaming.) Work up to ten minutes a day of this mindless mental wandering. Then start paying attention to your thoughts to see if a word or goal materializes. If it doesn't, extend the exercise to eleven minutes, then twelve, then thirteen . . . until you find the length of time you need to ensure that something interesting will come to mind. The Gaelic phrase for this state of mind is "quietness without loneliness."

Note that this activity is the exact opposite of meditation. You are not trying to empty your mind, not trying to sit restfully without conscious thoughts. You're seeking thoughts from the unconscious, and trying to tease them forward until you can latch onto them. An idea will sneak into your brain. Get engaged with that idea, play with it, push it around—you've acquired a goal to underpin this solitary activity. You're not alone anymore; your goal, your idea, is your companion.

Consider fishing, also a solitary activity. You have the gear and the equipment. You have the flies in the tackle box. You have the boat and the trip you have to take on the water to where the fish are biting. You have the casting over and over again, and the interior musings about how long it's going to take you to get a bite on the line. And you're doing this all by yourself for hours! What elevates it, what keeps it from turning into frightening drudgery, of course, is that you have a goal. You want to catch fish.

It's the same with daydreaming creatively—minus the tackle box, the boat, and the fish. You're never lonely when your mind is engaged.

Alone is a fact, a condition where no one else is around. Lonely is how you feel about that. Think of five things that you like to do all by yourself. It could be a hot bath, a walk up a favorite hill, that quiet moment of sinking into a chair with coffee when the kids have left for school. Refer back to the list whenever the aloneness of the creative process seems too much for you. The pleasant memories will remind you that *alone* and *lonely* are not the same thing.

Solitude is an unavoidable part of creativity. Self-reliance is a happy by-product.

3 Face Your Fears

It's not only Nature that abhors a vacuum; fear of empty space affects everyone in every creative situation. Where there was nothing, there will be something that has come from within you. That's a scary proposition. Putting a name to your fears helps cut them down to size.

When you sat in that brainstorming session at work, why didn't you speak up? When that idea for a story flitted through your mind, why didn't you seize it and pursue it? After you started drawing in that sketchbook, why did you stop?

I've told you my five big fears. Here are a few that might be yours:

I'm not sure how to do it: A problem, obviously, but we're not talking about constructing the Brooklyn Bridge. If you try and it doesn't work, you'll try a different way next time. Doing is better than not doing, and if you do something badly you'll learn to do it better.

People will think less of me: Not people who matter. Your friends will still love you, your children will still call you "mommy," your dog will still go for walks with you.

It may take too much time: Yes, it may, but putting it off isn't going to make it happen faster. The golfer Ben Hogan said, "Every day you don't practice you're one day further from being good." If it's something you want to do, make the time.

It will cost money: Are your creative efforts worth it to you? Is it something you really want to do? If so, make it your priority. Work around it. Once your basic needs are taken care of, money is there to be used. What better investment than in yourself?

It's self-indulgent: So? How often do you indulge yourself? Why shouldn't you? You won't be of much value to others if you don't learn to value yourself and your efforts.

These are some of the best, most paralyzing fears. If you examine your concerns closely, you should be able to identify and break down the ones that are holding you back. Don't run away from them or ignore them; write them down and save the page. There's nothing wrong with fear; the only mistake is to let it stop you in your tracks.

4 Give Me One Week Without

People go on diets all the time. If they don't like their weight, they stop eating certain foods. If their spending is out of control, they lock away their credit cards. If they need quiet time at home, they take the phone off the hook. These are all diets of one kind or another. Why not do the same for your creative health? Take a week off from clutter and distractions, such as these:

Mirrors: Go a week without looking in the mirror. See what happens to your sense of self. Instead of relying on the image you see reflected in a glass, find your identity in other ways. This forces you to stop looking at yourself so much and start focusing on others. You'll be forced to think more about what you do, and less about how you look. There's a difference between how you see yourself and how you think others see you; you might get confirmation back or you might be surprised. Either way, it's a discovery process. It's also a great technique for heightening your sense of curiosity. I guarantee that after a week without mirrors, you'll be dying to see yourself again. It could be a very interesting reintroduction. You might meet someone totally new.

Clocks: Put away your wristwatch. Shield your eyes from clocks. Stop relying on timepieces to gauge the passing of time. If you're engaged in what you're doing, time doesn't matter. It passes swiftly without notice. If you're not engaged, the clock will only depress you more. It tells you what you already know: You're in a rut and things aren't working. You don't need that negativity.

Newspapers: Stop reading newspapers and magazines for a week. I don't recommend this as a permanent diet; it eventually breeds ignorance. But one week won't do much damage. It's like going on vacation to a remote island, cut off from the usual media clutter. You may have done that already in your life. What have you lost? More important, what have you gained?

Speaking: I know a soprano who nearly ravaged her beautiful voice during a run of difficult opera performances. The cure was three weeks without speaking while her vocal cords recuperated. She enjoyed the self-imposed silence so much, she now has a no-speaking ritual for one week every year. It's not only a rest for her chief artistic muscle—her voice—it's also a stark reminder of the difference between what's worth saying and what isn't. It's the perfect editor for the creative soul.

Once you've done without these four, it's easy to come up with other distractions that invade your creative life without enhancing it. The telephone. The computer. The coffee shop. The car. The television (!). You get the idea. There are a lot of distractions out there—and you can live without them. At least for a little while.

your creative DNA

Chapter 3

In my early years in New York City, I studied with the choreographer Merce Cunningham. Merce had a corner studio on the second floor at 14th Street and Eighth Avenue, with windows on two sides. During breaks in classes, I watched a lot of traffic out of those windows, and I observed that the traffic patterns were just like Merce's dances—both appear random and chaotic, but they're not. It occurred to me that Merce often looked out of those windows, too. I'm sure the street pattern was consoling to him, reinforcing his discordant view of the world. His dances are all about chaos and dysfunction. That's his creative DNA. He's very comfortable with chaos and plays with it in all his work. My hunch is that he came to chaos before he came to that studio, but I can't help wondering if maybe he selected the place because of the chaos outside the windows.

Of course, when I looked out those windows, I didn't see the patterns the way Merce did, and I certainly didn't find solace in their discordance. I didn't "get it" the way he did. I wasn't hard-wired that way. It wasn't part of my creative DNA.

I believe that we all have strands of *creative code* hard-wired into our imaginations. These strands are as solidly imprinted in us as the genetic code that determines our height and eye color, except they govern our creative impulses. They determine the forms we work in, the stories we tell, and how we tell them. I'm not Watson and Crick; I can't prove this. But perhaps you also suspect it when you try to understand why you're a photographer, not a writer, or why you always insert a happy ending into your story, or why all your canvases gather the most interesting material at the edges, not the center. In many ways, that's why art historians and literature professors and critics of all kinds have jobs: to pinpoint the artist's DNA and explain to the rest of us whether the artist is being true to it in his or her work. I call it DNA; you may think of it as your creative hard-wiring or personality.

When I apply a critic's temperament to myself, to see if I'm being true to my DNA, I often think in terms of focal length, like that of a camera lens. All of us find comfort in seeing the world either from a great distance, at arm's length, or in close-up. We don't consciously make that choice. Our DNA does, and we generally don't waver from it. Rare is the painter who is equally adept at miniatures and epic series, or the writer who is at home in both historical sagas and finely observed short stories.

The photographer Ansel Adams, whose black-and-white panoramas of the unspoiled American West became the established notion of how to "see" nature (and, no small feat, helped spawn the environmental movement in the United States), is an example of an artist who was compelled to view the world from a great distance. He found solace in lugging his heavy camera on long treks into the wilderness or to a mountaintop so he could have the widest view of land and sky. Earth and heaven in their most expansive form was how Adams saw the world. It was his signature, an expression of his creative temperature. It was his DNA.

Focal length doesn't only apply to photographers. It applies to any artist.

The choreographer Jerome Robbins, whom I have worked with and admire, tended to see the world from a middle distance. The sweeping vision was not for him. Robbins's point of view was right there on the stage. Others besides me have noted how often Robbins had his dancers watch someone else dance. Think of his very first ballet, *Fancy Free.* Boys watch girls. Girls then watch boys. And upstage, the bartender watches everything as if he were Robbins's surrogate. His is the point of view from which the ballet's story is told. Robbins is both observing and observed, safely, at a middle distance.

It helps to know that Robbins grew up wanting to be a puppeteer, and I think this way of seeing the world—controlling events from behind the scenes or above, but not so distant that you cannot maintain contact with the action on stage—pervades almost everything he created. I doubt it was something he chose consciously, but in terms of creative DNA, it was a dominant strand in his work. Check out the film of *West Side Story,* which Robbins choreographed and co-directed. The story line is famously adapted from Shakespeare's *Romeo and Juliet*—in other words, it's not his own. Yet even with a borrowed plot, you still see Robbins's impulses coming to the fore, imprinting themselves on the drama and the dancing. Nearly every group scene involves performers being observed. Jets watch Sharks, Sharks watch Jets, girls watch boys, boys watch girls. This is not how Shakespeare did it. But it is Robbins's worldview.

Other artists see the world as if it is one inch from their nose. The novelist Raymond Chandler, whose Philip Marlowe books like *Farewell, My Lovely* and *The Long Goodbye* are classics of American hardboiled detective fiction, was obsessed with detail. He works in extreme close-up, a succession of tight shots that practically put us inside the characters' skulls. The plots of his stories are often incomprehensible—he believed that the only way to keep the reader from knowing whodunit was not to know yourself—but his eye for descriptive detail was razor-sharp. Here is the opening of his first full-length novel, *The Big Sleep:*

It was about eleven o'clock in the morning, mid October, with the sun not shining and a look of hard wet rain in the clearness of the foothills. I was wearing my powder-blue suit, with dark blue shirt, tie and display handkerchief, black brogues, black wool socks with dark blue clocks on them. I was neat, clean, shaved and sober, and I didn't care who knew it. It was everything the well-dressed private detective ought to be. I was calling on four million dollars.

Chandler kept lists of observed details from his life and from the people he knew: a necktie file, a shirt file, a list of overheard slang expressions, as well as character names, titles, and one-liners he intended to use sometime in the future. He wrote on half-sheets of paper, just twelve to fifteen lines per page, with a self-imposed quota that each sheet must contain what he called "a little bit of magic." The "life" in his stories was in the details, whether his hero Marlowe was idling in his office or in the middle of a brutal confrontation. No long-distance musings on the state of the world. No middle-distance group shots. Just a steady stream of details, piling one on top of the other, until a character or scene takes shape and a vivid picture emerges. Up close was Chandler's focal length. If some people like to wander through an art museum standing back from the paintings, taking in the effect the artist was trying to achieve, while others need a closer look because they're interested in the details, then Chandler was the kind of museum-goer who pressed his nose up to the canvas to see how the artist applied his strokes. Obviously, all of us look at paintings from each of these vantage points, but we focus best at some specific spot along the spectrum.

I don't mean to get too caught up in observational focal length. It's one facet out of many that makes up an artist's creative identity. Yet once you see it, you begin to notice how it defines all the artists you admire. The sweeping themes of Mahler's symphonies are the work of a composer with a wide vision. He sees grand architecture from a distance. Contrast that with a miniaturist like Satie, whose delicate compositions reveal a man in love with detail. (It's only the giants like Bach, Cézanne, and Shakespeare who could work in many focal lengths.)

But that's the point. Each of us is hard-wired a certain way. And that hard-wiring insinuates itself into our work. That's not a bad thing. Actually, it's what the world expects from you. We want our artists to take the mundane materials of our lives, run it through their imaginations, and surprise us. If you are by nature a loner, a crusader, an outsider, a jester, a romantic, a melancholic, or any one of a dozen personalities, that quality will shine through in your work.

Robert Benchley wrote that there are two kinds of people in the world: those who divide the world into two kinds of people, and those who don't. I guess I've always been one who does.

I have issues with ambiguity, preferring my distinctions to be black or white. I don't like gray. That's how I am. I recognize, of course, that some people do like gray. (I also recognize that I'm doing it again—dividing the world into two kinds of people.) Thus, I am always making these clear distinctions in my work, my daily routines, my colleagues, and my goals. Dancers are either acceptable (great) or not (everything less than great). Producers are either good or evil. Colleagues are either committed or missing in action. Critics are either my friends or enemies. The polar distinctions can go on forever.

If one set of polarities defines my creative DNA, it is the way I find myself pulled between *involvement* and *detachment.*

I shuttle back and forth from one extreme to the other, with no rest in between. And I apply it to everything.

With my dancers, for example, I have an annoying need for proof of their allegiance to me and my projects. So I'm always running through a mental checklist to see if their work habits are as exacting as mine, searching with forensic intensity for evidence of their commitment. Do they show up on time for rehearsal? Are they warmed up? Does their energy flag when rehearsals break down or are they committed to pushing forward? Are they bringing ideas to the party or waiting for me to provide everything? These are my personal pop quizzes to gauge other people's involvement. I don't want them merely involved. I'm looking for insane commitment.

I'm no less strict with myself. I'm always taking temperature readings of my commitment to a project and pushing myself to be more committed than anyone else. At its extreme, I put myself at the center of a piece, even as a dancer, trying on the roles.

When I've learned all I can at the core of a piece, I pull back and become the Queen of Detachment. I move so far back that I become a surrogate for the audience. I see the work the way they will see it. New, fresh, objectively. In the theater, I frequently go to the back and watch the dancers rehearse. If I could watch from farther away, from outside the theater in the street, I would. That's how much detachment I need from my work in order to understand it.

This impulse comes naturally. I grew up in the foothills of San Bernardino, where there was no community to speak of, no neighbors and playmates. I watched movies in a drive-in theater from a distance. I was even distanced from my twin brothers and my sister, who were all younger than I. They lived at one end of our house, I lived at the other so I could be free to maintain my rigorous practice schedule alone. You could even say I was detached from my world by my schedule. That's why detachment is part of my DNA. I was born with it, and it was continually drummed into me thereafter.

Was it there from the start? Who's to say, but my mother told me that at birth I was a noisy, ill-mannered baby in the hospital. The only way the nurses could shut me up was to put me out in the hallway by myself where I could see everything going on around me. I quieted down instantly. Even then, I didn't want to be on the inside, crowded with other people. I wanted to be on the outside, watching.

For the longest time, I thought this dichotomy of involvement versus detachment was merely a template for my work habits. Immerse yourself in the details of the work. Commit yourself to mastering every aspect. At the same time, step back to see if the work scans, if it's intelligible to an unwashed audience. Don't get so involved that you lose what you're trying to say. This was the yin and yang of my work life: Dive in. Step back. Dive in. Step back.

It was how I saw the world—like being nearsighted rather than having 20/20 vision. I was stuck with it.

And then one day, reading Carl Kerenyi's *Dionysos,* I discovered a broader context for these divisions. Involvement and detachment explained how I worked, but they didn't explain why I produced the work I did. It had always irked me that my dances shied away from telling a story, and when I tried my hand at a narrative-driven dance, the result was weak or unfocused. Why was that? Why was I better at one than the other? An answer came from the ancient Greeks, who had two words, *zoe* and *bios,* to distinguish the two competing natures I felt within myself.

Zoe and *bios* both mean life in Greek, but they are not synonymous. *Zoe,* wrote Kerenyi, refers to "life in general, without characterization." *Bios* characterizes a specific life, the outlines that distinguish one living thing from another. *Bios* is the Greek root for "biography," *zoe* for "zoology."

I cannot overstate what a profound distinction this was. Suddenly, two states of experience were made plain to me.

Zoe is like seeing Earth from space. You get the sense of life on the rotating globe, but without a sense of the individual lives being lived on the planet. *Bios* involves swooping down from space from the perch of a high-powered spy satellite, closing in on the scene, and seeing the details. *Bios* distinguishes between one life and another. *Zoe* refers to the aggregate.

Bios accommodates the notion of death, that each life has a beginning, middle, and end, that each life contains a story. *Zoe,* wrote Kerenyi, "does not admit of the experience of its own destruction: it is experienced without end, as infinite life."

The difference between *zoe* and *bios* is like the difference between sacred and profane. Sacred art is *zoe*-driven; profane art stems from *bios.*

I realize that these are just words. But they articulated a distinction that made my entire creative output clearer. Applying it to two of my choreographic heroes, Robbins and George Balanchine, I could appreciate in a new way the difference between these two men.

Balanchine was the essence of *zoe.* Most of his ballets are beautiful plotless structures that mirror the music rather than interpret it. They do not need language to explain themselves, nor do they try to tell a story. Their content is the essence of life, not the details of living. Balanchine's steps and gestures are not specific—for example, a man miming the act of pulling out an imaginary chair for a woman or, more tritely, putting hands to heart to express love. People think his dances are abstract at first—where's the story? what's the plot? But their *zoe* qualities reveal themselves with powerful results. Balanchine's gestures and steps pluck chords in us that we cannot easily name. Yet they resonate. They seem familiar. That's the genius of Balanchine. In his movement he created a grammar that expressed congruencies between the natural world and our emotional world. Three women unbundle their long hair at the end of *Serenade* and we feel something, without attaching a name to it, because there is a common structure between the dancers' gestures and some gesture we remember that moved us.

Robbins, on the other hand, was pure *bios*—and brilliant at it. When he created a dance, he was always accumulating details about the roles—from what the characters would wear to whom they were sleeping with—and out of these details of life he would construct an engaging narrative. This is why he had such a crowd-pleasing career in the theater. (This is a giant gift. Mike Nichols tells a story about getting the musical *Annie* ready for Broadway. A scene that was supposed to be funny was failing to get laughs, no matter what Nichols tried. He asked Robbins to watch the scene with his practiced eye. Afterward, Nichols asked him how to fix the scene. Robbins surveyed the stage and pointed to a white towel hanging at the back of the set. "That towel should be yellow," he said. "That's it?" thought Nichols. "That makes the scene work?" But he made the change and the scene got a laugh every night thereafter.)

As a man of *bios*, a master of details, he could tell a story that had, as a subtext, what Balanchine made a text of—namely, life.

One approach was not more valid than the other. The two men simply entered their work through different doors.

But I could see that everything I did was a duel between the warring impulses of *bios* and *zoe* in me. On the one hand, there was my ability to create dances about a life force. On the other, there was my occasional urge to break away from this and create dances that tell a specific story. The first kind of dances came naturally to me, the latter required more of an effort. In my heart I am a woman more of *zoe* than of *bios*.

I suspect many people never get a handle on their creative identity this way. They take their urges, their biases, their work habits for granted. But a little self-knowledge goes a long way. If you understand the strands of your creative DNA, you begin to see how they mutate into common threads in your work. You begin to see the "story" that you're trying to tell; why you do the things you do (both positive and self-destructive); where you are strong and where you are weak (which prevents a lot of false starts), and how you see the world and function in it.

Take the following questionnaire. If even one answer tells you something new about yourself, you're one step closer to understanding your creative DNA. There are no right or wrong answers here. The exercise is intended for your eyes only, which means no cheating, no answers to impress other people. It's supposed to be an honest self-appraisal of what matters to you. Anything less is a distortion. I include it here and urge you to answer quickly, instinctively. Don't dawdle.

(To get you started, I give you my answers on pages 54 to 59.)

Your Creative Autobiography

1. What is the first creative moment you remember?

2. Was anyone there to witness or appreciate it?

3. What is the best idea you've ever had?

4. What made it great in your mind?

5. What is the dumbest idea?

6. What made it stupid?

7. Can you connect the dots that led you to this idea?

8. What is your creative ambition?

9. What are the obstacles to this ambition?

10. What are the vital steps to achieving this ambition?

11. How do you begin your day?

12. What are your habits? What patterns do you repeat?

13. Describe your first successful creative act.

14. Describe your second successful creative act.

15. Compare them.

16. What are your attitudes toward: money, power, praise, rivals, work, play?

17. Which artists do you admire most?

18. Why are they your role models?

19. What do you and your role models have in common?

20. Does anyone in your life regularly inspire you?

21. Who is your muse?

22. Define muse.

23. When confronted with superior intelligence or talent, how do you respond?

24. When faced with stupidity, hostility, intransigence, laziness, or indifference in others, how do you respond?

25. When faced with impending success or the threat of failure, how do you respond?

26. When you work, do you love the process or the result?

27. At what moments do you feel your reach exceeds your grasp?

28. What is your ideal creative activity?

29. What is your greatest fear?

30. What is the likelihood of either of the answers to the previous two questions happening?

31. Which of your answers would you most like to change?

32. What is your idea of mastery?

33. What is your greatest dream?

I devised this questionnaire because it forces us to go back to our origins, our earliest memories, our first causes. We change through life, but we cannot deny our sources, and this test is one way to recall those roots.

The better you know yourself, the more you will know when you are playing to your strengths and when you are sticking your neck out. Venturing out of your comfort zone may be dangerous, yet you do it anyway because our ability to grow is directly proportional to an ability to entertain the uncomfortable.

I've always admired the playwright Neil Simon. In economic terms and mass acceptance, he's probably the most successful playwright of the twentieth century. He wrote beautifully constructed parlor comedies that provided a laugh every twenty seconds. That was his gift, and it was a rare talent. I'm sure there are snobs who tried to dismiss Neil Simon as a joke mechanic producing a hit a year. I don't see it that way. I look over his enormous output—three dozen plays, a dozen original screenplays—and see a paragon of habitual creativity. More to the point, I see a writer constantly stretching. He pushed his talent more than most people appreciate. He didn't go against his nature and try to write dramas like Eugene O'Neill—he was too smart for that—but he was always injecting into his plays dark elements and serious themes that tested his abilities and made his audience stretch, too. Where his strengths for comedy could cover his experiments, his stretches, he knew he could go for it. There is a large gap in time and ambition between *Barefoot in the Park* in 1961 and the Pulitzer Prize–winning *Lost in Yonkers* in 1990. But both plays are recognizably Neil Simon. He had a good sense of who he was and how far he could venture beyond his comfort zone.

Another thing about knowing who you are is that you know what you should not be doing, which can save you a lot of heartaches and false starts if you catch it early on.

I was giving a lecture to students at Vassar not long ago. Working with the students' autobiographies, I invited a dance student, a music student who brought his saxophone, and an art student to join me on stage. I asked the dancer to improvise some movement from a tuck position on the floor. I asked the saxophone player to accompany the dancer. And I asked the art student to assign colors to what they were doing. I admit I was constructing a three-ring circus in the lecture hall. But my goal was to bring the three students together by forcing them to work off the same page, and also to free them up to discover how far they could go improvising on this simple assignment.

When I asked the art student to read out loud his color impressions, everyone in the hall was taken aback. He droned on and on about himself, feelings he'd had, stories about friends. Not a word about color. Finally I heard "limpid blue" come out of his mouth. I waved my arms, signaling him to stop reading.

"Do you realize," I said, "that you've just recited about five hundred words in an assignment about color. You've covered everything under the sun, and 'limpid blue' is the first time you've mentioned a color? I'm not convinced you want to be a painter."

As far as I was concerned, this young man was in "DNA denial." I gave him a painterly exercise and he gave me a text-heavy response. A young man with painting in his genes would be rattling off colors immediately. Instead, his vivid use of language—limpid blue does not come in tubes—suggested that he really ought to be a writer.

It would be presumptuous of me to think I had him pegged for a writer, not a painter, after that brief encounter. But if I got him to re-examine what he's built for, then he was a step or two ahead of most people.

I had a similar moment in my early years as a choreographer. I was at my worktable making sketches of dancers and their costumes. As I leaned back to admire the sketches, there was a fleeting moment when I actually whispered to myself "I could have been a painter."

I wonder how many people get sidetracked from their true calling by the fact that they have talent to excel at more than one artistic medium. This is a curse rather than a blessing. If you have only one option, you can't make a wrong choice. If you have two options, you have a fifty percent chance of being wrong.

It's like a great high school athlete who plays football, basketball, and baseball equally well. If this athlete wants to continue playing sports at the highest collegiate level, at some point he will have to commit to one sport over the others. He'll weigh a lot of factors: what comes naturally to him, what does he enjoy the most, in which sport does he have a natural advantage over the competition in terms of size, speed, endurance, and other critical measures? But in the end the choice should be based on pure instinct and self-knowledge. What sport does he feel in his muscles and bones? What sport was he born to play?

In my case, I fortunately banished the "I could have been a painter" thought out of my mind as quickly as it had appeared. Maybe I did have a talent for interpreting the world visually. Maybe I did have a knack for creating visual tableaus that entertained people. Maybe I did know how to arrange colors and objects in space. All of these are skills from the painter's tool kit. But even then I knew myself well enough to realize that no matter how much I enjoyed making sketches, the painter's life was not for me. I didn't feel it in my bones. I would tell my "story" through movement. Gotta dance.

exercises

5 You Can Observe a Lot by Watching

Yogi Berra said that, and it's true. Go outside and observe a street scene. Pick out a man and woman together and write down everything they do until you get to twenty items. The man may touch the woman's arm. Write it down. She may run her hand through her hair. Write it down. She may shake her head. He may lean in toward her. She may pull away or lean in toward him. She may put her hands in her pockets or search for something in her purse. He may turn his head to watch another woman walking by. Write it all down. It shouldn't take you very long to acquire twenty items.

If you study the list, it shouldn't be hard to apply your imagination to it and come up with a story about the couple. Are they friends, would-be lovers, brother and sister, work colleagues, adulterers, neighbors who run into each other on the street? Are they fighting or breaking up or falling in love or planning a weekend together or debating which movie they want to see? The details on your list provide plenty of material for a short story, but that's not the goal of this exercise.

Now do it again. Pick out another couple. This time note only the things that happen between them that you find *interesting,* that please you aesthetically or emotionally. I guarantee that it will take you a lot longer to compile a list of twenty items this way. You might need all day. That's what happens when you apply *judgment* to your powers of observation. You become selective. You edit. You filter the world through your particular prism.

Now study the two lists. What appealed to you in the second, more selective list? Was it the moments of friction between the couple or the moments of tenderness? Was it the physical gestures or their gazes away from each other? The varying distance between them? The way they shifted their feet, or leaned up against a wall, or took off their glasses, or scratched their chins?

What caught your fancy is not as important as the difference between the two lists. What you included and what you left out speaks volumes about how you see the world. If you do this exercise enough times, patterns will emerge. The world will not be revealed to you. *You* will be revealed.

6 Pick a New Name

Imagine you could change your name. What would you choose? Would it be a name that sounded good or belonged to someone you admire? Would it make a statement about what you believe or how you want the world to approach you? What would you want it to say about you?

This is not just an exercise in "what if." It's about identity—who you are and aim to be.

I've always thought my creative life began the moment my mother named me Twyla. It's an unusual name, especially when you combine it with Tharp. (Twyla Smith just doesn't have the same ring, does it?) My mother had seen the name "Twila" in a clipping about the queen of a hog-calling contest in Indiana, and as she explained it, "I changed the *i* to a *y* because I thought it would look better on a marquee." She had big plans for me. She wanted me to be singular, so she gave me a singular name.

If it's a parent's job to make children feel special, then my mother did her job well. To me, the name is fierce, independent, and unassailable. It can't be shortened to Twy or La, and it doesn't take a diminutive well. (I have a good friend who always adds an affectionate Yiddish "leh" to names, but "Twylaleh" is too much even for him.) It's a good name to have if you want to leave your mark in the world.

More than anything, though, my name is original. It makes me strive for originality—if only to live up to the name.

I am not exaggerating the magic and power invested in our names. Names are often a repository of a kind of genetic memory. Parents, who are the arbiters of all given names, certainly feel the power; that's why they name their children after ancestors (or themselves). They honor those who came before while connecting their child with his or her past. The hope is that not only will some of our forebears' genes pass down with the name, but also their courage, their talents, their drive, and their luck. (We named our son Jesse Alexander, after my grandfather Jesse Tharp and my husband's grandfather Alexander Huot, because we admired their work ethic and their skill at building things. I figured if their genes were funneling into my son, he ought to get the names that go with them. Interestingly, Jesse is happiest when he is building things.)

The essayist Joseph Epstein has noted, "A radical change in one's name seems in most cases a betrayal—of one's birthright, of one's group, of one's identity." I don't agree. In a sense it's a commitment to a higher personal calling. And it's not uncommon among creative souls.

The ancient masters of Japanese art were allowed to change their name once in their lifetime. They had to be very selective about the moment in their career when they did so. They would stick with their given name until they felt they had become the artist they aspired to be; at that point, they were allowed to change their name. For the rest of their life, they could work under the new name at the height of their powers. The name change was a sign of artistic maturity.

Mozart played with variations on his name for most of his life. He was baptized Joannes Chrysostomus Wolfgangus Theophilus Mozart. His father Leopold referred to him shortly after his birth as Joannes Chrisostomus Wolfgang Gottlieb. The young Mozart generally referred to himself with the middle name Amadè or Amadé (Gottlieb, Theophilus, and Amadeus being German, Greek, and Latin, respectively, for "lover of God"). But he made a significant change at the time of his marriage to Constanze Weber: In all documents related to the marriage (except for the marriage contract itself), his name is given as "Wolfgang Adam Mozart." By taking the name of the first man, Mozart may have been declaring himself reborn, set free from the past. "Mozart's constant alterations of his name are his way of experimenting with different identities," wrote Mozart biographer Maynard Solomon, "trying to tune them to his satisfaction."

The boxer Cassius Clay changing his name to Muhammad Ali is one of the great creative acts of the twentieth century. Cassius Clay was already the heavyweight champion of the world, but converting to Islam, throwing off the shackles of a slave name, and becoming Ali gave him an even larger identity for a much bigger stage. It helped make him the most famous person on earth.

Done wisely and well, a change of name can be a self-fulfilling prophecy. As Epstein points out, "Eric Blair, Cicily Fairfield, and Józef Teodor Konrad Korzeniowski became, respectively, George Orwell, Rebecca West, and Joseph Conrad—the first to shuck off the social class into which he was born, the second to name herself after a feminist heroine in Ibsen, the last to simplify his name for an English audience. Yet how right those names now seem, how completely their owners have taken possession of them!"

My Creative Autobiography

1. What is the first creative moment you remember? Sitting in my mother's lap at the keyboard, listening to notes.

2. Was anyone there to witness or appreciate it? I got lots of validation and feedback all through my early years, as most kids do when they're being taught something difficult and they have to improve every day. My piano teacher was always pasting "seals of approval" on my lesson books, everything from gold stars to black stars to decals of rabbits and other farm animals. What I really remember though is the sponge my teacher used to wet the decals and stick them on my lesson books. She kept the sponge in a little jar on the side of the keyboard, and as I played, I always had my eye on the sponge. That sponge was not only the symbol of my reward, it was the tool for administering it. I felt connected to it in a special way. I loved that sponge. And I loved my little blue books that contained all my stars. I still have them. So, yes, someone was always around to see my little acts of creativity.

3. What is the best idea you've ever had? To follow my own course in life and become a dancer, because dancing was what I did best. I wasn't as good at anything else.

4. What made it great in your mind? I went with my gut, not my head. Dance is a tough life (and a tougher way to make a living). Choreography is even more brutal because there is no way to carry our history forward. Our creations disappear the moment we finish performing them. It's tough to preserve a legacy, create a history for yourself and others. But I put all that aside and pursued my gut instinct anyway. I became my own rebellion. Going with your head makes it arbitrary. Going with your gut means you have no choice. It's inevitable, which is why I have no regrets.

5. What is the dumbest idea? Thinking I could have it all.

6. What made it stupid? Its built-in futility, given how I work. To lead a creative life, you have to sacrifice. "Sacrifice" and "Having it all" do not go together. I set out to have a family, have a career, be a dancer, and support myself all at once, and it was overwhelming. I had to learn the hard way that you can't have it all, you have to make some sacrifices, and there's no way you're going to fulfill all the roles you imagine. We thought, as women in the sixties and seventies, that we could change everything and remake all the rules. Some things changed, and some things pushed back. What makes it stupid is that I set up a way of working that was in direct conflict with my personal ambition. Something had to give.

7. Can you connect the dots that led you to this idea? I was a senior alone in a dressing room, next to a dance studio. I was in a discussion with myself, and it had been going on for four years, ever since my sophomore year when I left Pomona College to go to Barnard College in New York City (the heart of the dance world). I looked at my body in the dressing room mirror and, in that moment, I saw the potential for a dancer. As I was changing into practice clothes, I felt as if I were putting on a uniform, and I thought, "Yes, I want to join this team." That's when and how I made my life choice.

8. What is your creative ambition? To continually improve, so I never think "My time may be over."

9. What are the obstacles to this ambition? The pettiness of human nature. Mine as well as others'.

10. What are the vital steps to achieving this ambition? I often think of

myself as water flowing into a rock. The water eventually finds its way out the other side, but in between it seeks out every hole and channel in the rock. It keeps trickling forward, gathering force until it bursts out on the other side as a raging torrent. That's my career experience. I don't have steps or ladders. I don't improve in steps. I'm the water slapping into the rocks. I gather force and then . . . explode.

11. How do you begin your day? I wake at 5:30 A.M., head across town for a workout at the gym (for fourteen years with the same trainer, Sean Kelleher).

12. What are your habits? What patterns do you repeat? I repeat the wake-up, the workout, the quick shower, the breakfast of three hard-boiled egg whites and a cup of coffee, the hour to make my morning calls and deal with correspondence, the two hours of stretching and working out ideas by myself in the studio, the rehearsals with my dance company, the return home in the late afternoon to handle more business details, the early dinner, and a few quiet hours of reading. That's my day, every day. A dancer's life is all about repetition.

13. Describe your first successful creative act. When I was eight, living in San Bernardino, California, I was always forced to practice alone in my room. But I wanted human contact and some commentary on what I was doing. So I would gather the kids in the neighborhood and convince them to come with me into the back canyons where we lived, and there I would design theatrical initiations for the kids. This was my first creative act, my first moment of being a floor general and moving people around. My first choreography.

14. Describe your second successful creative act. Sixteen years later, my first concert, *Tank Dive*, 1965.

15. Compare them. They're the same. In both I'm organizing people in time and space with a ritualistic intent.

16. What are your attitudes toward:

Money? Hate that I need it.

Power? Challenge it if you don't have it. Don't abuse it if you do.

Praise? Don't trust it.

Rivals? Bless them.

Work? What I live for.

Play? Work.

17. Which artists do you admire most? Mozart, Bach, Beethoven, Balanchine, and Rembrandt.

18. Why are they your role models? They aspired, they approached, they matured. They passed "Go" more than once. Their work ended up light-years beyond where they started.

19. What do you and your role models have in common? Total commitment. I strive to follow their example. I try to emulate their staying power and constant growth. I am different because *I am a woman*. There is a big difference between how a male artist gets to live and what the world expects of a woman, artist or not.

20. Does anyone in your life regularly inspire you? Maurice Sendak. I talk to him every Sunday, and he always provides the best chuckle of the week. He's the only person with whom I can just *blurt*, uncensored. And he does the same thing. We're like two wicked children. It's a delight. Dick Avedon also inspires me because of his ongoing discipline, his ongoing ambition, his ongoing efforts at self-education, and his ongoing grace. He has real ingenuity. Even when he's using old solutions he's still inventive.

21. Who is your muse? **My dancers.**

22. Define muse. **That for whom you long to labor.**

23. When confronted with superior intelligence or talent, how do you respond?
Enthusiastically. I can get there. Let's go.

24. When faced with stupidity, hostility, intransigence, laziness, or indifference in others, how do you respond?
Stupidity: Run, don't walk.
Hostility: Get nicer.
Intransigence: Push back.
Laziness: See Stupidity, above.
Indifference: Move on.

25. When faced with impending success or the threat of failure, how do you respond?
Success: With relief.
Failure: More work, *fast*.

26. When you work, do you love the process or the result? **I love to study the beginnings of things. The first steps are the most interesting ones—when you're just beginning to find your way into a problem, whether it's artistic or philosophical, and when you don't yet know what you're trying to solve and how you're going to solve it. To me there's something very solid about the first time something is**

achieved. I know when I'm working that the very first time I get something right it's righter than it will ever be again. I cheated on the answer: I love the process—all the time. I love the result—the first time.

27. At what moments do you feel your reach exceeds your grasp? I always, always feel that at the start. But you get lucky now and again, so I reach anyway. That's why I study beginnings, so I can deal with those fears.

28. What is your ideal creative activity? Dancing well.

29. What is your greatest fear? That I won't be able to do it.

30. What is the likelihood of either of the answers to the previous two questions happening? Possible and inevitable, in that order.

31. Which of your answers would you most like to change? Number six. Down deep, I still want to have it all.

32. What is your idea of mastery? Having the experience to know what you want to do, the vision to see how to do it, the courage to work with what you're given, and the skill to execute that first impulse—all so you can take bigger chances.

33. What is your greatest dream? To be paid on the same level as professional athletes and pop stars. This would mean I live in a world where dance is as popular as soccer or rock 'n' roll. If the luckiest people in the world are the ones who get paid for doing what they would otherwise do for free, I am already lucky. But I'm an optimist. My greatest dream is always to be luckier.

Chapter 4

harness your memory

When Homer composed the *Iliad* and *Odyssey,* he was drawing on centuries of history and folklore handed down by oral tradition. When Nicolas Poussin painted *The Rape of the Sabine Women,* he was re-creating Roman history. When Marcel Proust dipped his petites madeleines into his tea, the taste and aroma set off a flood of memories and emotions from which modern literature has still not recovered.

There are as many forms of memory as there are ways of perceiving, and every one of them is worth mining for inspiration.

Memory, as we most frequently think of it, encompasses every fact and experience that we can call up at will from our cranial hard drives. We all have this in varying abundance. It's the skill that lets us store away the vital and seemingly trivial data and images and experiences of our lives. I say vital and seemingly trivial, but I really don't distinguish between the two. To some people, vital information is their best friend's phone number. To someone else, it's the lyrics to the "Catalog Aria" from *Don Giovanni* or Rick's airport speech from *Casablanca* or a recipe for couscous.

I spend a lot of time worrying about memory. One of the horrors of growing older is the certainty that you will lose memory and that the loss of vocabulary or incident or imagery is going to diminish your imagination.

As a result, I try to give my memory a workout, training it to keep it sharp. When I watch a rehearsal or performance of one of my dances, I strive to remember the first twelve to fourteen notes or corrections I want to discuss with the cast without writing them down. That's my limit—twelve to fourteen notes— which is nothing to sneeze at. Most people can't recall much more than three notes in any context. Think about the last lecture you heard or business meeting you attended or book you had to read. How many of the important take-away points could you recall if you didn't memorialize them in writing?

I don't just try to remember the notes in an unconnected list; I sort them in my mind by category, remembering comments I want to make performer by performer, or scene by scene, remembering them by associating them with space, time, and music. The act of categorizing serves as a memory aid itself, as does ticking off the notes on my fingers. If I know that I have fourteen notes, I'll be able to recall them through the associated muscle memory of the finger gestures as I count them out. I work a lot faster if I can walk into rehearsal the next day and rattle off my changes to the performers off the top of my head instead of consulting some pieces of paper. It also gives me authority. Think about the last time you were the only person in a room who remembered a salient fact. What did that do for your credibility at that precise moment? Memory has that power.

But thinking of memory only in this way is simplistic. It shrinks our minds down to the size and sophistication of a personal computer—a machine defined and priced by how much it can remember and how quickly it can retrieve information. Creativity has little to do with this kind of memory. If it did, the most creative people would have hair-trigger memories of photographic proportions, and our artists would all be found slaughtering the competition on *Jeopardy!*

Just because you can recite Shakespeare's sonnets from memory doesn't mean you have the poetic spark to write a sonnet of your own.

Creativity is more about taking the facts, fictions, and feelings we store away and finding new ways to connect them. What we're talking about here is metaphor. Metaphor is the lifeblood of all art, if it is not art itself. Metaphor is our vocabulary for connecting what we're experiencing now with what we have experienced before. It's not only how we express what we remember, it's how we interpret it—for ourselves and others.

When Shakespeare's Macbeth asserts in eleven quick lines that life is a "brief candle," that life is a "walking shadow," that life is "a poor player," and finally that life is "a tale told by an idiot, full of sound and fury, signifying nothing," we take his meaning immediately because we can call up memories of candles, of shadows, of players, and of tales told by idiots. This is how lines written four hundred years ago connect with us today. They not only play on our memory, they rely on it.

Metaphor, as Cynthia Ozick writes, "transforms the strange into the familiar. This is the rule even of the simplest metaphor—Homer's wine-dark sea, for example. If you know wine, says the image, you will know the sea."

If all art is metaphor, then all art begins with memory. The ancient Greeks knew this: In their origin myths, they cite Mnemosyne, the goddess of memory, as the mother of the Nine Muses.

To fully appreciate the authority of memory, you need to appreciate the more exotic forms of memory lurking on the fringes. You remember much more than you may think you do, in ways you haven't considered.

Muscle memory is one of the more valuable forms of memory, especially to a performer. It's the notion that after diligent practice and repetition of certain physical movements, your body will remember those moves years, even decades, after you cease doing them. In the dance world, muscle memory comes into play every day; we couldn't survive without it. Unlike musicians or actors, who have sheet music and scripts to study, dancers have nothing written down. It's all in their heads and bodies. We'd have to start rehearsal from step one every day if our muscles didn't remember. What's amazing is how long dancers' bodies retain the information. Let's say I asked Rose Marie Wright, a dancer with whom I worked thirty years ago, to teach dances she performed for many years to another generation of dancers. If she demonstrates the dance without thinking about it, she will re-create each step and gesture perfectly on the spot the first time, as though she were a medium in a trance. That's muscle memory. Automatic. Precise. A little scary. The second time through, however, or trying to explain the steps and patterns to the dancers, she will hesitate, second-guess herself, question her muscles, and forget. That's because she's thinking about it, using language to interpret something she knows nonverbally. Her memory of movement doesn't need to be accessed through conscious effort.

Learning steps is only one demonstration of the muscles' intelligence. A virtuoso pianist is doing the same thing when he sits down at the keyboard and dashes off a piece of music he hasn't thought about in years. He has practiced and played the piece so many times in the past, that the memory has never left him. It resides in the parts of his brain that govern his fingers and his muscles, not the parts he would use to ponder this sentence.

Muscle memory has its uses in the creative process, perhaps more for acquiring skill than for developing inspiration. But it's useful nevertheless. I know one novelist who taught himself the craft of fiction by retyping the stories of his favorite authors. The act of typing someone else's words—rather than simply reading them—made him stop and think about how the author chose words, constructed sentences and paragraphs, arranged dialogue, and structured a narrative. In this case, the exercise is less about muscles and more about perceiving structures and harmonies anew—from the vantage point of the author rather than the reader.

Raymond Chandler and Proust went through a similar process when honing their very different crafts. Chandler believed Hemingway to be the greatest

American novelist of his time, and he wrote imitations of Hemingway's style to absorb what he loved about it. Proust went further, spending twelve years translating and annotating the writing of the English art historian John Ruskin. He also wrote a series of articles for *Le Figaro* imitating the styles of such nineteenth-century literary figures as Balzac and Flaubert.

It's no different from a young person sitting with a drawing pad in a museum copying a great artist. Skill gets imprinted through the action.

If there's a lesson here it's: get busy copying. That's not a popular notion today, not when we are all instructed to find our own way, admonished to be original and find our own voice at all costs! But it's sound advice. Traveling the paths of greatness, even in someone else's footprints, is a vital means to acquiring skill.

When I started out as a dancer in New York, I became obsessed with studying every great dancer who was working at the time and patterning myself after him or her. I would literally stand behind them in class, in copying mode, and fall right into their footsteps. Their technique, style, and timing imprinted themselves on my muscles.

That's one of the ways I learned to dance. I'm not sure how much impact it had on my choreography, because I didn't end up creating dances like anyone else. But, like a writer who writes more vividly because he has a huge vocabulary, or a painter who excels because of exquisite draftsmanship, I needed to hone my dancing skills in order to create. If I couldn't dance well, how would I have the authority to tell others how to dance, or know what a good dance was?

That's the power of muscle memory. It gives you a path toward genuine creation through simple re-creation.

There are more flamboyant examples of memory, such as virtual memory, which is the ability to project yourself into feelings and emotions from your past, and to let them manifest themselves physically. Actors do this all the time—every blush or flow of tears that's ever touched you in a movie results from a performer who's learned to mine the past. Actors train themselves to travel back to that beach ten years ago and feel the temperature and the air, to find a link between then and now and use it to give detail and personal resonance to a scene.

You can even project your virtual memory into the future. Some business-people do this as an exercise in visualization, imagining the ending of a sensitive negotiation as a means to achieving the desired result. They remember what a successful deal feels and sounds like, and they call that imagery up, seeing everyone in the room smiling and shaking hands, then they retrace their steps to see how they got there, and how they can get there again. The flamboyant Cuban chess master José Capablanca, world champion through most of the 1920s, envisioned how the game would end and improvised his way to that point. The French ski champion Jean-Claude Killy, I'm told, was a master at this. If he was recovering from an injury and couldn't take his practice runs the days before a race, he would rely on his memory of the mountain and picture himself racing the entire course. He would do this repeatedly until he felt the course implanted in his muscles. This gave him the feel of success.

Then there's **sensual memory**, where the sudden appearance of a smell or taste or sound or color instantly floods the imagination with images from the past. One taste of those madeleine crumbs and Proust is suddenly embarking on his monumental *In Search of Lost Time* (previously translated as *Remembrance of Things Past*). We've all experienced sensual memory, whether it's the smell of oatmeal cookies hurtling us back to our childhood or the opening notes of a song that induces reveries (or nightmares) of who we were with the last time we heard it. This is potent stuff, and it's there to be used.

There's also memory that arises from your environment. Businesses, for example, are set up in a way that gives people far greater access to the inspirational power of memory than they realize. One of the more successful executives I know once told me that whenever he was feeling stale or creatively stalled at work, he'd read the contents of four- or five-year-old files. This seemingly mundane act of poring through old correspondence and memos never failed to spark an idea or, at least, lift him out of his funk. The name of a forgotten colleague or customer would fly off the page of a musty letter and set his brain in motion. Like an actor doing sensory exercises, he'd picture the customer in his mind: what he looked like, how he talked, the reasons they met, the details of his business, the people they knew in common. The simple act of trying to recall the customer would open up a torrent of memories and associations. And in that torrent he'd inevitably find a useful idea.

He even had a name for the space he was tapping into: **institutional memory**. As he told me, "Look, it's very rare to come across something truly original in a corporate environment. Most, if not all, of your good ideas are probably sitting somewhere in your files or are locked up in the brains of the people who have worked at your company for years. In other words, the good ideas are institutionalized. They exist and they're yours for the taking. All you've got to do is find a way to tap into them. To me, that means (a) digging through files and (b) really listening to the people who've worked here a long time. They know a lot more than anyone thinks. Hell, they don't even know how much they remember until you ask them."

Whether he knew it or not, the executive was on to something profound and slightly ironic. While most people in the workplace—and in the arts—think they have to be constantly looking forward to be edgy and creative, this man found that the real secret of creativity is to *go back and remember.*

Of all the forms of memory, **ancient memory** is the one that interests me most. That helps explain why this dispatch from Seth Mydans in the *New York Times* in March 2002 caught my eye. It was a story about the Cambodian dancer Sina Koy and how her homeland has influenced her life and art.

"We believe our ancestors are watching us, even if we do not see them," Sina Koy said. "It was because of the spirits of the ancestors inside me that I became a dancer." Not long ago she visited the ancient temples of Angkor and studied the stone bas-reliefs where dancers bend and turn and float just as they do today on the broad bare stage of the practice hall. Seeing them, Sina Koy understood that nothing had changed. Everything that she does today was done then.

I understand exactly what she feels. I once saw a news photograph of an ancient dance artifact. It was a pottery shard with a design showing a tribal migration that was believed to be the earliest known representation of dance. It gave me a twinge, if not a shock, of recognition. I felt as though I have that illustrated moment stored in me genetically or else I wouldn't be a dancer. That's ancient memory. This is not Jungian voodoo; it's real. This first graven image of these dancers gives me an intense feeling of déjà vu. The memory is not only ancient, it's ancestral. I felt proud. If you have ever danced in a group, those people on the pottery are your forebears.

This kind of notion is tricky to put into words, particularly when the memory we're dealing with is nonverbal and involves a physical movement. But I know there are many moments in my working day when I sit back and ask myself, How do I know that this particular creative decision on the dance floor, going from x to y, is right? What makes me so sure I'm making the right choice? The answer I whisper to myself is often nothing more than "It feels right." And part of the reason it feels right is that the move has been reinforced in us over centuries of practice. Every dance I make is a dive into this well of ancient memory.

In the case of the pottery design, the shock of recognition was so jolting that it gave me the spine for a new dance, in a process that went something like this:

The first thought that came to mind when I saw the ancient figures was the idea of migration. So I started thinking of a piece that would tell a story of people migrating from one place to another. Migrations move in many directions, but to the American mind raised on Manifest Destiny they move from east to west. So that westerly direction became the guiding metaphor for the dance: I would move the dancers across the stage east to west (or stage left to stage right as I defined it) and the audience would literally watch them migrate from one side to the other.

The notion of migration prompted images of people who were disadvantaged, politically and economically. After all, that's why people uproot themselves and travel great distances: They're escaping peril, suffering, and oppression. Thoughts of oppression led me to consider the blues as music for the piece, because blues is the signal expression of pain and suffering in our musical heritage.

All these thoughts sprang to mind in a matter of seconds. I was bequeathed a new dance, complete with story line and structure and music, simply by the ancient memory of the first dancers. It was exhilarating.

It didn't work out that easily. I spent hours at my worktable and in the studio tackling the first challenge—moving a group of "migrant" dancers across the stage in a vague approximation of the Conestoga wagons traveling across the

American West. I sketched. I fooled around with my coin exercise (see page 109). But no matter what I tried, I couldn't find a scheme to move the dancers interestingly across the stage. Everything I tried looked like I was rolling a lumpy human ball from stage left to stage right.

The music was no less vexing. I spent $800 on CDs by Ray Charles, B. B. King, and Van Morrison and listened to them. Nothing clicked. Eventually a friend, seeing me lost in the blues, turned me on to violinist Mark O'Connor, whose bluesy, jazzy fiddle playing promised to be a perfect fit for my conception. O'Connor (bless him) had written a piece so sweeping and lush and romantic— ten times more Aaron Copland than B. B. King—that it could never be mistaken for the blues.

In the end, the piece, a fourteen-minute high-energy celebratory romp, now known as *Westerly Round,* bore absolutely no resemblance to my original notion. With the migration metaphor fallen by the wayside and the blues soundtrack abandoned, I gave up the sad story line as well. The only idea that survived and made it to the stage were the linked hands of the dancers. I used the hand-holding as a controlling image in the piece for three boys and a girl. If it felt right to the artist drawing the figures on the pottery, it felt right to me as well. Ancient memory was at work.

Once you realize the power of memory, you begin to see how much is at your disposal in previously underappreciated places. The trick is figuring out how to tap into it. You can't always wait for a photo of an ancient pot to appear in the Science section of the *New York Times* and jolt you into action. Sometimes you have to be proactive about mining the veins of memory within you.

Maybe it's because I was an art history major whose basic education was how to look, but I am magnetically drawn to images, whether they're paintings, photographs, film, or video. They are all lodestones of inspiration to me.

In my senior year, when I was torn between my art studies and a consuming urge to dance, I used to comfort myself by camping out in the Dance Collection of the New York Public Library.

I'm not sure what motivated me to do this. It wasn't as if I woke up one day and announced, "Okay, I'm going to look at dance pictures today." But I was an art student, looking at photographs of paintings and sculpture all day long and believing that everything in a picture was there for a reason. It was only logical that one day I asked myself, Why aren't I looking at pictures of dance? That's what I'm really interested in. So I did.

The New York Public Library houses one of the world's great dance archives. I asked the curator to bring me photos of the women pioneers of dance: Isadora Duncan, Ruth St. Denis, Doris Humphrey, Martha Graham. I could read their movement vocabulary from those photographs, keeping what was useful to me and ignoring what wasn't. I would slide my hands over the plates, trying to connect with how they moved by how they looked frozen in time. It had nothing to do with their faces or makeup or clothes—nothing connected to their glamour or my vanity. I was trying to absorb how their bodies worked, taking their movement potential out of their bodies and imprinting it on my own, just as I did every day in class as I worked in the footsteps of great dancers.

A famous picture of Doris Humphrey nude in a circle, though obviously posed, fascinated me because she totally lacked self-consciousness. I could clearly see what her body was doing and I could see what obvious relish she took in fulfilling that position in the circle. Her feeling of pride also imprinted itself on me. I would pore over a Martha Graham picture so intently that I could gauge the size of her footsteps or feel her body's tension as she torqued inside her costume.

If a picture is a memory captured, then these great dance photos helped me capture a new memory. The archival images came to me through my eyes and I absorbed them first in my brain, then in my body, and finally in my own memory. Once they were locked in me, I was free to call on them anytime.

If one day I was stuck, I could ask myself, How would Martha move? or What would Doris Humphrey feel like? I could harness their memory as easily as if it were my own, and use the things they were using to fashion my own solutions.

In a sense, I was apprenticing myself to these great women, much as Proust had to Ruskin and Chandler to Hemingway. A young friend of mine recently described an internship he was about to begin. He called the process "shadowing," following around a mentor and learning from him. That's what I was doing in the archives, shadowing my predecessors. This is how you earn your ancestry.

exercises

7 Name That Muse

Here's an exercise in associative memory for you: below, I've listed the nine muses, those brilliant and charming and vexing daughters of Zeus and Mnemosyne who held sway over the classical arts. You can remember them through fierce application of direct rote repetition, or you can attach to each some image or memory that the name or subject triggers as you look at the list. The latter works better; you might even find yourself honoring their mother by inventing a little memory aid or ditty—a *mnemonic*—to bring the nine names to mind.

Calliope	Epic poetry
Clio	History
Erato	Love poetry and lyric poetry
Euterpe	Music
Melpomene	Tragedy
Polyhymnia	Sacred song
Terpsichore	Dance and choral song
Thalia	Comedy
Urania	Astronomy

How would I remember the nine names? *Can clear, earnest effort make proper things total up?* That might help—the first letters of the nine words in that last sentence match the first letters of the names of the muses. But how do you associate each with her field?

The easy ones are Urania (sounds like the planet Uranus, hence astronomy), Polyhymnia (*hymns* are sacred songs), and Erato (*eros* means love). What do the other six remind you of? Can you connect them to their domains? And what types of memory do you use in calling forth those images?

74

Remembering the muses is no shortcut to creative bliss, though it will make crossword puzzles easier and classicists smile. And perhaps this nod in their direction will cause them to visit you when you need their help.

8 Trust Your Muscle Memory

For this exercise, you'll have to come up with a simple set of discrete moves. Don't worry if you've never invented movement before; you're testing your body's memory, not choreographing for Broadway. (And don't try to fink out by claiming you have no space. Push the furniture back. Create a small space patch and get to work.) Take a set of ten moves: for example, raise your right arm, lift your left foot, drop the left foot, pivot 180 degrees to your right on your left foot, drop the right arm. Putting your hands on your hips, bend forward from the waist, then straighten up. Now turn 180 degrees to your right on your left foot and scoot forward on both feet.

This is a phrase. Repeat it five times the first day, four the second, three the third, two the fourth, and once the fifth. Now don't do it for a week. But do think about it several times, picturing it in your mind during the course of the week. After one week, start the phrase by lifting the right arm. Now continue without thinking about what comes next. Let the body go on its own.

You may be surprised by how much you (or your muscles) remember.

Once you have seen the power of muscle memory, try this exercise: Flail about for ten seconds, and don't think about it afterward. Can you repeat your flailing pattern tomorrow? Next time, *do* think about your flailing. Play the motions back in your mind. Think about the rhythms, in real time, in your imagination. Now, tomorrow, see if you can retrieve this flailing pattern any better than the first. You are learning how to *train* your muscle memory, your ability to retain and repeat motion.

Your muscles are smarter than you think.

9 Mining for Memory in a Photograph

I'm always amused when people show me baby pictures. I love how much information and meaning, not to mention joy, they extract from a clumsy, poorly composed snapshot of a four-week-old child's smiling face. In that face they can see a universe of inherited features and family resemblances—the eyes that come from their mother, the family chin passed down from a paternal grandfather, the brow and hairline that inarguably foretell premature baldness. Frankly, I don't see it.

It's another story when the picture involves me.

No picture has more resonance for me than this early snapshot with my mother. It helps to know the impact my mother had on my creative life, which in many ways was total and all-consuming. From naming me Twyla, to playing piano scales for me when I was three months old (to train my ear), to driving me thirty thousand miles a year

throughout my youth to the finest teachers in Southern California (so I could study piano, baton, ballet, toe, flamenco, drums, elocution, painting, viola, violin, shorthand, German, and French), she built me step by step for a creative life. It helps to be aware of this when you look at the girl, age two, in her short dress (obviously a dance costume, no?). It connects to much more than my early years. It hooks me up to an intravenous line of mnemonic fluid, explaining my identity and providing the source as well.

Let me tell you what I see in this picture.

I see a little person here, very excited about the idea of stepping out into the real world. A little shy about it, actually, which is why she holds only one of her mother's fingers. It's not as if there is a real person here yet. This person—me—is a bicycle with training wheels, a person in a suspended state of yet-to-be.

I love the two stones behind the girl, a perfect platform constructed by my father, suggestive of an ancient Greek amphitheater. Conceivably, this could be my first stage photo. Note the left foot slightly forward. It's as if the girl has stepped off a stage and is just beginning to address an audience.

I also like the mischief in the girl's face, head slightly bowed, eyes shyly turned up but looking straight ahead. There's a feeling of anticipation and curiosity here, as if she's standing in front of a door and is about to walk through.

There's also zest and dynamic energy in the girl. She wants to *go.*

I like the one finger of Mother's hand. It could be perceived as tentative, as if the child needs assistance. But I remember it differently. The one finger is about as little as I could hold on to without going solo. It's as if the girl is saying "I'd really rather be doing this by myself. But I can't quite yet."

I also like the period details: the short haircut (still stylish to me), the short dress baring dancer's legs, the shoes and socks cut off because they would lack finesse and destroy the line. As for Mother being cropped out of the picture . . . well, let's not go there.

This photo reminds me of how every young person grows up with an overwhelming sense of possibility, and how life, in some ways, is just a series of incidents in which that possibility is either enlarged or smacked out of you. How you adapt is your choice. In that sense, this photo is Darwinian: It's the origin of species. And I'm the species.

More than anything, though, to me, this is the photo of a girl standing in front of the door . . . before she kicks it in. It summarizes me. If I ever have an identity crisis, this picture will cure it.

Now it's your turn. Take a family picture, any picture, and study it. What do you see in it that is indisputably similar to your life today, to the person you've become? What is vaguely similar? What bears no resemblance or suggests nothing memorable? What ended up the opposite of what you see? Why these four different outcomes? Explain this to yourself. In doing so, note the people and events that spring to mind. What faces—relatives, friends, teachers, neighbors, nemeses, strangers, pets—appear unbidden? When was the last time you thought of these people? That's memory, and it's buried in everything you've saved, patiently waiting for you to dislodge it and, hopefully, use it.

It's like poring through your high school yearbook. Who can look at yearbook photos without a swell of such emotions as nostalgia, regret, isolation, pleasure? The exercise here with a family photo is much the same. The goal is to connect with something old so it becomes new. Look and imagine.

before you can think out of the box,

you have to start with a box

Everyone has his or her own organizational system. Mine is a box, the kind you can buy at Office Depot for transferring files.

I start every dance with a box. I write the project name on the box, and as the piece progresses I fill it up with every item that went into the making of the dance. This means notebooks, news clippings, CDs, videotapes of me working alone in my studio, videos of the dancers rehearsing, books and photographs and pieces of art that may have inspired me.

The box documents the active research on every project. For a Maurice Sendak project, the box is filled with notes from Sendak, snippets of William Blake poetry, toys that talk back to you. I'm sure this is the sort of stuff that most people store on shelves or in files. I prefer a box.

There are separate boxes for everything I've ever done. If you want a glimpse into how I think and work, you could do worse than to start with my boxes.

The box makes me feel organized, that I have my act together even when I don't know where I'm going yet.

It also represents a commitment. The simple act of writing a project name on the box means I've started work.

The box makes me feel connected to a project. It is my soil. I feel this even when I've back-burnered a project: I may have put the box away on a shelf, but I know it's there. The project name on the box in bold black lettering is a constant reminder that I had an idea once and may come back to it very soon.

Most important, though, the box means I never have to worry about forgetting. One of the biggest fears for a creative person is that some brilliant idea will get lost because you didn't write it down and put it in a safe place. I don't worry about that because I know where to find it. It's all in the box.

I like cardboard file boxes for a bunch of reasons, all willfully idiosyncratic. The shelving in my work area at home, which holds my audio equipment, hundreds of music CDs, and piles of musical scores, is not mere heavy-gauge industrial shelving; it's scaffolding equipment, strong enough for painters to stand on when they're working on the exterior of a house. In other words, the shelves are built for hard work. That's a personal aesthetic choice. I want everything around me, from my dancers to my dances to my shelves, to be strong and built to last.

The file boxes reflect the same practicality. They're easy to buy, and they're cheap. (I don't need to spend a thousand dollars on an exquisite cherry cabinet that fills up in a week.) They're one hundred percent functional; they do exactly what I want them to do: hold stuff. I can write on them to identify their contents (you wouldn't do that with a thousand-dollar cherry file cabinet). I can move them around (which is also hard to do with a heavy wood filing system). When one box fills up, I can easily unfold and construct another. And when I'm done with the box, I can ship it away, out of sight, out of mind, so I can move on to the next project, the next box.

Easily acquired. Inexpensive. Perfectly functional. Portable. Identifiable. Disposable. Eternal enough.

Those are my criteria for the perfect storage system. And I've found the answer in a simple file box.

It's not the only answer, of course. Maurice Sendak has a room that's the equivalent of my boxes, a working studio that contains a huge unit with flat pullout drawers in which he keeps sketches, reference materials, notes, articles. He works on several projects at a time, and he likes to keep the overlapping materials out of sight when he's tackling any one of them. Other people rely on carefully arranged index cards. The more technological among us put it all on a computer. There's no single correct system. Anything can work, so long as it lets you store and retrieve your ideas—and never lose them.

It doesn't have to be complicated. I know one magazine editor who hoards newspaper and magazine clippings. A good chunk of his day is spent with scissors in hand clipping stories, photographs, and illustrations. After he clips, he opens a file drawer and deposits the clippings on a pile of other clippings. Then he closes the drawer, letting them accumulate in the drawer's cool darkness. He doesn't think about them much, but he knows they are there if needed, which happens whenever a colleague wanders into his office desperate for a good idea. He'll open the drawer again, haul out its contents on his desk, and say, "Let's see what we've got here." Host and guest then leaf through the clippings together. Without fail, an intriguing headline or phrase or photo of someone will beget a thought that in turn suggests a story idea—and the guest will depart, slightly less desperate and infinitely more inspired. The drawer, in effect, contains the editor's pre-ideas—those intriguing little tickles at the corners of your brain that tell you when something is interesting to you without your quite knowing why. Bringing them out reminds him of what he was thinking when he put them there in the first place.

I also like the simplicity of a box. There's a purpose here, and it has a lot to do with efficiency. A writer with a good storage and retrieval system can write faster. He isn't spending a lot of time looking things up, scouring his papers, and patrolling other rooms at home wondering where he left that perfect quote. It's in the box.

A perfect archive also gives you more material to call on, to use as a spark for invention. Beethoven, despite his unruly reputation and wild romantic image, was well organized. He saved everything in a series of notebooks that were organized according to the level of development of the idea. He had notebooks for rough ideas, notebooks for improvements on those ideas, and notebooks for finished ideas, almost as if he was pre-aware of an idea's early, middle, and late stages.

For anyone who reads music, the sketchbooks literally record the progress of his invention. He would scribble his rough, unformed ideas in his pocket notebook and then leave them there, unused, in a state of suspension, but at least captured with pencil on paper. A few months later, in a bigger, more permanent notebook, you can find him picking up that idea again, but he's not just copying the musical idea into another book. You can see him developing it, tormenting it, improving it in the new notebook. He might take an original three-note motif and push it to its next stage by dropping one of the notes a half tone and doubling it. Then he'd let the idea sit there for another six months. It would reappear in a third notebook, again not copied but further improved, perhaps inverted this time and ready to be used in a piano sonata.

He never puts the ideas back exactly the same. He always moves them forward, and by doing so, he re-energizes them.

The notebooks are remarkable for many reasons. Beethoven was a volatile and restless personality, always demanding a change of scene. In the thirty-two years he lived in and around Vienna, he never bought a home and moved more than forty times. I suspect that's why he needed the elaborate system of notebooks. With all the turmoil in his personal life, the notebooks anchored the one part of his life that mattered: composing. As long as he had his ideas captured on paper, his creativity would never waver. In fact, it got stronger.

That's the true value of the box: It contains your inspirations without confining your creativity. Let me explain how.

In the summer of 2000 I had an idea: to make a Broadway musical, all dancing, to the songs of Billy Joel. I have always believed in Billy's music. I've been listening to his songs since he started recording. I also felt in my bones that he wrote great dancing music. At the same time, I had just started a new company of six marvelous dancers, so good, in fact, that I was dying to showcase them in something big and ambitious. A two-hour dance extravaganza to all the hits of a major American pop idol fit the bill.

Only trouble was, I didn't know Billy Joel. I had never met him. I didn't know if he was an egomaniac or a bored rock star or a cool guy open to something new. On the evidence of his songs, which were literate and told great stories, he seemed like a down-to-earth good guy. That was his reputation. I got his phone number and called him up. I said, "I have a project in mind and I would like to show you something." The "something" I had in mind was a twenty-minute videotape of choreography I had prepared to some of his music.

(The tape was a critical piece of preparation, and vital to selling the idea to the two people who could make or break the project. The first person was me: I had to see that Billy's music could "dance." The tape was visual evidence of something I felt. The second person, of course, was Billy. That's why I called him the moment I was sure. I have learned over the years that you should never save for two meetings what you can accomplish in one. The usual routine for selling an idea is you set up a first meeting to explain it and then a second meeting to show it. I didn't want to leave anything to chance. Who knew if I would ever get a second meeting? When busy people are involved, a lot of things can happen to foul up even well intentioned plans, so I decided to go for it all in one shot and invested my time and money into producing and editing the twenty-minute tape.)

When Billy came to my home on Manhattan's Upper West Side, I mentioned that I had a little trouble figuring out both from his songs and the surname Joel whether he was Jewish, Irish, or Italian. He said, "My family is Jewish, I grew up in an Italian neighborhood, and every girl who broke my heart was Irish."

I said, "Okay, I get it now. Come and look"—and I pulled him over to my video console.

I showed him some dancing to his newest compositions—solo piano music from his classical *Fantasies and Delusions* album—because I assumed he would be most engaged by his most recent material. He loved the dancing. Then I switched to his rock hits such as "Uptown Girl" and "Big Shot." He said, "I didn't know my stuff could look so good." End of tape.

I think he was flattered by it all, so I pressed on. I asked him, "Whatever happened to Brenda and Eddie from the song 'Scenes from an Italian Restaurant'?"

He said he had never thought about it.

"Well, that's the point," I said. "I want to do a show using your songs to tell a story. I don't know what it is yet. But first, I need your permission."

He said, "Okay, you have it."

"I'm also going to need access to your entire song catalog."

He said, "Fine."

That was it. It was one of those rare moments: an instant deal. We shook hands and he left.

That's the moment I started my Billy Joel box for the show *Movin' Out.*

First in: my precious twenty-minute tape.

Next in: two blue index cards. I believe in starting each project with a stated goal. Sometimes the goal is nothing more than a personal mantra such as "keep it simple" or "something perfect" or "economy" to remind me of what I was thinking at the beginning if and when I lose my way. I write it down on a slip of paper and it's the first thing that goes into the box.

In this case, I had two goals. The first was "tell a story." I felt that getting a handle on narrative in dance was my next big challenge, plus I wanted to find out what happened to Brenda and Eddie, the "popular steadies." The second was "make dance pay for the dancers." I've always been resentful of the fact that some of the so-called elite art forms can't survive on their own without sponsorship and subsidies. It bothers me that dance companies around the world are not-for-profit organizations and that dancers, who are as devoted and disciplined as any NFL or NBA superstar, are at the low end of the entertainment industry's income scale. I wanted this Broadway-bound project not only to elevate serious dance in the commercial arena but also to pay the dancers well. So I wrote my goals for the project, "tell a story" and "make dance pay," on two blue index cards and watched them float to the bottom of the Joel box. Along with the tape, they were the first items in the box and they sit there as I write this, covered by months of research, like an anchor keeping me connected to my original impulse. ("When you're up to your ass in alligators," says a friend from Florida, "it's easy to forget that your objective was to drain the swamp.")

No matter what system you use, I recommend having a goal and putting it in writing. I read once that people who write down their New Year's resolutions have a greater chance of achieving them than people who don't. This is the sort of factoid that is probably apocryphal but, like many urban legends, sounds as though it should be true.

Into the box went all my research. A few days after we met, Billy sent his complete CDs. I listened to them in chronological order over the weekend, and by Monday I had the first hints of a story line running through my head. It was the opening line of Homer's *Iliad:* "Sing to me muse of the rage of Achilles." Billy was my Homer figure, the poet reciting an epic poem. The story would be set to twenty-seven Billy Joel songs about five kids from Long Island, from their high school days in 1965 through the Vietnam War and ending in 1984. The main characters—Eddie, Brenda, Tony, James, and Judy—could all be found in Billy's songs. I studied Billy's music videos for clues and meaning lurking in the songs. I watched tapes of his live performances through the years. I looked at TV dance shows from the era—such as *Shindig* and *Soul Train*—to refresh my memory of the dance styles back then. I screened Billy's lectures to hear what he thought of his songs. All these items went into the box. Because the show's story line included a pivotal section about the Vietnam War, I went to New York's Museum of Television and Radio to watch news footage, refreshing my memory of what we were told during the war. Then I watched the movies about the Vietnam War, from *The Deer Hunter* to *Platoon* to *Apocalypse Now* and *Full Metal Jacket.* All into the box, along with seminal books from the time period (for example, Michael Herr's *Dispatches*) and interesting period films (such as *Saturday Night Fever* and even one I worked on, *Hair*). I went back farther to study *The Wild Ones* and *Rebel Without a Cause* to get a feel for an older character in our show who'd wear a black leather jacket and motorcycle boots. All in the box. From another box, abandoned and buried, I dug out old research for an unrealized film project based on David Rabe's *In the Boom Boom Room* to develop ideas for a female character.

In the box you'll also find my **notebooks** containing all the clips and images and scrawls to myself that I file away to jog my memory: photos of Billy from the early seventies to the mid-eighties; news clippings from the period helping me formulate a visual style; song lists, from first cut to final cut, and the notes passed between music director Stuart Malina and me about why a song should or shouldn't be in the show. For example, there's an elaborate set of notes on a beautiful ballad from an early part of Billy's career, "She's Got a Way About Her," that is full of innocence and sweetness. But in my notes you can see the song morphing into something harsher, eventually becoming two simultaneous sleazy bar scenes, one in Vietnam, the other back home. I felt obliged to run this by Billy, warning him, "This is going to destroy the song." But he wasn't worried. "Go for it," he said.

Also in the box is a green beret that belonged to a military adviser I consulted for the show. He gave me some worthwhile information for the night patrol sequence, about how the men signaled to each other down the line, because the thickness of the jungle made it impossible to see more than one man along in the fanned-out formation. The signals were quite elementary (pointing to one's eyes means "look," fist lifted at a right angle means "stop," hand out flat pushing down means "get down"); we could have invented something equivalent for the scene, but real details created authenticity. Just seeing the beret in the box energizes me, reminding me how important it was to the man who gave it to me.

There are **tchotchkes** in the box as well, all of which link me to some essential aspect of the project. A pair of earrings and a macramé vest that started me thinking about costumes. Books about psychedelic light events that I might share with the lighting designer. Photographs of other production concepts that I could use to discuss space and detail with Santo Loquasto, my longtime production designer. There are research Polaroids from a reconnaissance trip to half a dozen village greens in Long Island where Billy Joel grew up. All of this helped me imagine the characters in their time and space when I started work in my pristine white studio in Manhattan. Eventually, the material for this show filled up twelve boxes.

That's how a box is like soil to me. It's basic, earthy, elemental. It's home. It's what I can always go back to when I need to regroup and keep my bearings. Knowing that the box is always there gives me the freedom to venture out, be bold, dare to fall flat on my face. Before you can think out of the box, you have to start with a box.

Now, let me tell you what a box isn't.

The box is not a substitute for creating. The box doesn't compose or write a poem or create a dance step. The box is the raw index of your preparation. It is the repository of your creative potential, but it is not that potential realized.

When a journalist gets a story assignment, he doesn't immediately sit down and knock out a finished piece. He has a routine, which is common to all good journalists. First, he reads all the background material he can get his hands on. Then he talks to people to verify old information, unearth new information, and pull out lively quotes (which he knows are the lifeblood of solid reporting). He jots all this down in his notes. Filling up the notebook can take hours or months, depending on the journalist's deadline. But only when his research and reporting are done and his notebook is full does he write the story. If his reporting is good, the writing will reflect that. It will come out clearly and quickly. If the reporting is shoddy, the writing will be, too. It will be torture to get the words out.

My box is like the journalist's notes. It's the "reporting" routine I follow before creating a piece. If the quality of a journalist's work is a direct function of how much background material he sifted through, how many people he talked to, how many times he went back to his sources to challenge or check up on their statements—that is, how diligent and clever he was in assembling his research—then the quality of my creative output is also a function of how diligent and clever I've been in filling up my boxes.

It's one thing to tell you that my *Movin' Out* box has dozens of videotapes of Billy Joel performances and music videos. That's obvious; if you're working with the man's music, you ought to know how that music has been treated visually in the past. That's the bare minimum in research. It's also basic research to review relevant films from the era. But I'm not sure everyone would log time reviewing U.S. Army training films from the Vietnam era. That's the mildly over-the-top research that tells me I'm prepared—and arms me with confidence when I get down to the real work of creating.

Sadly, some people never get beyond the box stage in their creative life. We all know people who have announced that they've started work on a project—say, a book—but some time passes, and when you politely ask how it's going, they tell you that they're still researching. Weeks, months, years pass and they produce nothing. They have tons of research but it's never enough to nudge them toward the actual process of writing the book. I'm not sure what's going on here. Maybe they're researching in the wrong places. Maybe they like the comfort zone of research as opposed to the hard work of writing. Maybe they're just taking procrastination to a new extreme. All I know for sure is that they are trapped in the box.

My solution for them: This isn't working. Free yourself. Get out of this box. Put it away for another day and start a new box. But do so with the faith that nothing is lost, that you haven't put in all this effort for naught. Everything you've done is in the box. You can always come back to it.

There's one final benefit to the box: It gives you a chance to look back. A lot of people don't appreciate this. When they're done with a project, they're relieved. They're ready for a break and then they want to move forward to the next idea. But the box gives you the opportunity to reflect on your performance. Dig down through the boxes archaeologically and you'll see a project's beginnings. This can be instructive. How did you do? Did you get to your goal? Did you improve on it? Did it change along the way? Could you have done it all more efficiently?

I find the box is most useful at three critical stages: when you're getting going, when you're lost, and after you've finished (that's when you can look back and see the directions you didn't take, the ideas that intrigued you but didn't fit this time around and might be the start of your next box).

Above all, learn to respect your box's strange and disorderly ways. As a repository of half-baked inspirations and unformed aids, the box can seem to be a haphazard tool while you're filling it. But when you want to go back and make sense of your path, every step is there to be found, and the order emerges if only in hindsight. Your box is proof that you have prepared well. If you want to know how any creative project will turn out, your box's contents are as good a predictor of success or failure as anything I know.

exercise

10 "Begin!"

My friend Irving Lavin, a Renaissance scholar at Princeton's Institute for Advanced Study, confessed that he had a horrible time writing because he never knew the beginning. Then he figured out that the paper's beginning was not the same as beginning to write. So he just started writing about an important point in the paper and trusted that he'd find the beginning eventually. Chekhov, when asked by a nephew how he knew where to start, replied, "Take your blue book and tear it in half. Begin there."

There's a difference between a work's beginning and starting to work.

I learned this with one of my earliest dances, *The Fugue.* Being a novice choreographer, I didn't know how to begin. So I stood up in the center of the room, took a deep breath, stamped my foot, and shouted "Begin!" Stamping the foot led me to think of the piece as tap dancing. The sound of my shoe against the floor gave me the idea of performing the piece in silence on an electronically amplified stage. To this day that's how *The Fugue* starts out—with a stomp that rings in my mind "Begin!"

I guess that's the real secret to creative preparation. If you're at a dead end, take a deep breath, stamp your foot, and shout "Begin!" You never know where it will take you.

91

scratching

Chapter 6

The first steps of a creative act are like groping
in the dark: random and chaotic, feverish and
fearful, a lot of busy-ness with no apparent or
definable end in sight. There is nothing yet to
research. For me, these moments are not pretty.
I look like a desperate woman, tortured by the
simple message thumping away in my head:
"You need an idea." It's not enough for me to
walk into a studio and start dancing, hoping
that something good will come of my aimless
cavorting on the studio floor. Creativity doesn't
generally work that way for me. (The rare times
when it has stand out like April blizzards.)
You can't just dance or paint or write or sculpt.
Those are just verbs. You need a tangible idea
to get you going. The idea, however minuscule,
is what turns the verb into a noun—paint into a
painting, sculpt into sculpture, write into
writing, dance into a dance.

Even though I look desperate, I don't feel desperate, because I have a habitual routine to keep me going.

I call it scratching. You know how you scratch away at a lottery ticket to see if you've won? That's what I'm doing when I begin a piece. I'm digging through everything to find something. It's like clawing at the side of a mountain to get a toehold, a grip, some sort of traction to keep moving upward and onward.

Scratching takes many shapes. A fashion designer is scratching when he visits vintage clothing stores, studies music videos, and parks himself at a sidewalk cafe to see what the pedestrians are wearing.

A film director is scratching when she grabs a flight to Rome, trusting that she will get her next big idea in that inspiring city. The act of changing your environment is the scratch.

An architect is scratching when he walks through a rock quarry, studying the algebraic connections of fallen rocks or the surface of a rock wall, or the sweeping space of the quarry itself. We see rocks; the architect sees space and feels texture and assesses building materials. All this sensory input may yield an idea.

You can scratch through books. I once walked into the office of a four-star Manhattan chef and his assistant as they were scouring through an enormous pile of international cookbooks, none of them in English as far as I could tell, obviously looking for menu ideas. They had a dazed, sheepish look in their eyes— dazed because I had interrupted them as they were zoning out in their pursuit of a good idea, sheepish because no one likes to be caught in the act of scratching.

Scratching can look like borrowing or appropriating, but it's an essential part of creativity. It's primal, and very private. It's a way of saying to the gods, "Oh, don't mind me, I'll just wander around in these back hallways . . ." and then grabbing that piece of fire and running like hell.

I'm often asked, "Where do you get your ideas?" This happens to anyone who is willing to stand in front of an audience and talk about his or her work. The short answer is: everywhere. It's like asking "Where do you find the air you breathe?" Ideas are all around you.

I hesitate to wax eloquent about the omnipresence of ideas and how everything we need to make something out of nothing—tell a story, design a building, hum a melody—already resides within us in our experience, memories, taste, judgment, critical demeanor, humanity, purpose, and humor. I hesitate because it is so blindingly obvious. If I'm going to be a cheerleader for the creative urge, let it be for something other than the oft-repeated notion that ideas are everywhere.

What people are really asking, I suspect, is not "Where do you get your ideas?" but "*How* do you get them?"

To answer that, you first have to appreciate what an idea is.

Ideas take on many forms. There are good ideas and bad ideas. Big ideas and little ideas.

A good idea is one that turns you on rather than shuts you off. It keeps generating more ideas and they improve on one another. A bad idea closes doors instead of opening them. It's confining and restrictive. The line between good and bad ideas is very thin. A bad idea in the hands of the right person can easily be tweaked into a good idea.

I like the following exchange between the movie producer Art Linson and the writer David Mamet, as Linson recorded it in his book of Hollywood tales, *What Just Happened?*:

> *The first rule of producing is to find a writer with an idea, or get an idea and find a writer. Since David Mamet and I had done* The Untouchables *together we'd developed a good professional working relationship: You get me a lot of money, I get you a good script.*
> *I placed the call: "Hi, Dave."*
> *"What's the shot?" he asked.*
> *"I got a new deal. I'm looking for you to write a new script."*
> *"Fine."*
> *"There'll be lots of money."*
> *"Good. Let's do it."*
> *"It's not that easy."*
> *"Why?"*

"Because if you don't tell me what it's about I can't get you the money."

"Fine. What do you want it to be about?"

"I don't know, that's why I'm calling you."

"I understand."

"Dave, how about an adventure movie?"

"Fine."

"Something castable. Two guys, maybe."

"Fine."

"C'mon, Dave, I need more to go on."

"O.K. . . . How 'bout two guys and a bear?"

"It's a start."

In Hollywood, an adventure movie with two guys doesn't quite qualify as an idea. Two guys and a bear does. It adheres to the unshakable rule that you don't have a really good idea until you combine two little ideas. Like all good ideas, it kept moving forward, eventually evolving into the movie *The Edge* with Anthony Hopkins and Alec Baldwin.

The difference between good and bad ideas is a lot like E. M. Forster's distinction between narrative and plot. Plot is "The queen died; the king died." Narrative is "The queen died; the king died of a broken heart." One man's bear is another's brokenhearted king. That is all you need to know about good ideas and bad.

The more useful comparison involves big ideas and little ideas.

You (and by "you" I mean both you and me, dear reader) don't scratch for big ideas. They come upon you mysteriously, unbidden, sometimes unwelcome (especially when they become impossible to execute). There is always an ulterior motive behind a big idea, usually that you want to catch people's attention, or make a pile of money, or both. Big ideas are self-contained and self-defining projects. I get them once or twice a year whenever I start to fret about the impermanence of my craft and want to make something enduring. I want people to remember I was here.

For me, a big idea is thinking I can film, preserve, and archive all my dances and calling it the "Decades" project. A big idea is waking up one day and telling myself I want to make a Broadway musical to the songs of Billy Joel. They are big ideas because they take up a lot of space in my mind, and if I commit to them, they will be all-consuming. They are big ideas because, in and of themselves, they are meaningless, little more than a goal or a dream; they cease to exist if I fail to follow up on them with the steady string of small ideas that make each a reality. For the musical, if I can't figure out a way to speak to Billy Joel and get his cooperation, if I can't select the right songs, if I can't construct a recognizable story line to tie the songs together, if I can't create the dance steps and find the best dancers and persuade people with money to back the show, and so on and so on with thousands of other daily sparks and imaginings and choices . . . then the big idea quickly shrivels and evaporates into nothing.

That is why you scratch for little ideas. Without the little ideas, there are no big ideas.

Scratching is what you do when you can't wait for the thunderbolt to hit you. As Freud said, "When inspiration does not come to me, I go halfway to meet it." How is that different from a movie producer calling up a gifted writer and prodding him to suggest a plot line of "two men and a bear"? If you go halfway, you double your chances of getting a toehold on an idea.

Remember this when you're struggling for a big idea. You're much better off scratching for a small one.

In *Zen and the Art of Motorcycle Maintenance,* Robert Pirsig describes an experience he had teaching rhetoric to college students in Bozeman, Montana. One girl, a serious and disciplined student often described by her teachers as lacking creativity, wanted to write a five-hundred-word essay about the United States. Pirsig opined that this was rather broad, and suggested that she narrow it to the town of Bozeman. When the paper came due, she arrived empty-handed and very upset, explaining that she'd tried but that she couldn't think of anything to say.

Pirsig next advised that she narrow it further to the main street of Bozeman. Again, she came in without an essay and in obvious distress. This time,

> *he told her angrily, "Narrow it down to the* front *of* one *building on the main street of Bozeman. The Opera House. Start with the upper left-hand brick."*
>
> *Her eyes, behind the thick-lensed glasses, opened wide. She came in the next class with a puzzled look and handed him a five-thousand-word essay on the front of the Opera House on the main street of Bozeman, Montana. "I sat in the hamburger stand across the street," she said, "and started writing about the first brick, and the second brick, and then by the third brick it all started to come and I couldn't stop."*

When you're in scratching mode, the tiniest microcell of an idea will get you going. Musicians know this because compositions rarely come to them whole and complete. They call their morsels of inspiration lines or riffs or hooks or licks. That's what they look for when they scratch for an idea.

It's the same for me. A dance doesn't hit me whole and complete. Inspiration comes in molecules of movement, sometimes in nanoseconds. A quick combination of three steps is an idea. A turn of the foot coupled with an arm gesture is an idea. A new way of collapsing to the floor is an idea. A man grabbing a woman above the elbow is an idea. A quick combination of five steps leading into a jump is practically a mega-idea—enough to keep me going for hours.

When I'm scratching I'm improvising. Like a jazz musician jamming for an hour to find a few interesting notes, a choreographer looks for interesting movement. I didn't start out knowing this; it came to me over time, as I realized that I would never get to the essential core of movement and dance through a cerebral process. I could prepare, order, organize, structure, and edit my creativity in my head, but I couldn't think my way into a dance. To generate ideas, I had to *move*. It's the same if you're a painter: You can't imagine the work, you can only generate ideas when you put pencil to paper, brush to canvas—when you actually do something physical.

Here's how I learned to improvise: I played some music in the studio and I started to move. It sounds obvious, but I wonder how many people, whatever their medium, appreciate the gift of improvisation. It's your one opportunity in life to be completely free, with no responsibilities and no consequences. You don't have to be good or great or even interesting. It's you alone, with no one watching or judging. If anything comes of it, you decide whether the world gets to see it. In essence, you are giving yourself permission to daydream during working hours.

I suppose this is no different from a songwriter noodling around at the keyboard waiting for a corpuscle of music to emerge and engage the ear, or a painter dashing off sketches right and left until one pleases the eye. That's what improvising is like for me. There's no tollbooth between my impulse and my action. I just do it and I consider the results, the consequences, and the truth (if any) later in repose. That's an incredible place to be. If you're privileged enough to be able to do that for forty-five minutes a few days a week, you have been given something wonderful.

There was one big problem with my improvisation: I couldn't see the results. A painter has those sketches littering the floor to look at later. A writer can read what's been written. A composer can jot down the notes that enticed his ear. I didn't have a way to capture my improvising when I started out (this was the 1960s, before the invention of portable video). It bothered me that I was wasting a lot of good movement in the studio. So I trained myself, through muscle memory, to remember my improvised steps. I called it going into "capture mode." Then I realized that I was defeating the purpose of improvisation, because once I asked my mind to *retain,* it was no longer free to improvise *without inhibition.* They were opposed activities, freezing me in place. The act of retaining defeated the purpose of scratching, which was to stop my conscious mind and mental filters from blocking my creative impulses.

I want to be clear here. When I talk about turning off the conscious mind and mental filters, I am not talking about meditating or mining the subconscious. Scratching is real and tangible. It bloodies your fingernails. The key is not to block yourself; you have to leave yourself open to everything. When he needed an idea, Thomas Edison liked to sit in a "thinking chair" holding a metal ball bearing in each palm, with his hands closed. On the floor, directly under his hands, were two metal pie pans. Edison would close his eyes and allow his body to relax. Somewhere between consciousness and dreaming his hands would relax and open without effort, letting the ball bearing fall noisily into the pie pans. That's when he would wake up and write down whatever idea was in his head at that moment. It was his way of coming up with ideas without his conscious mind censoring them.

The Harvard psychologist Stephen Kosslyn says that ideas can be acted upon in four ways. First, you must *generate* the idea, usually from memory or experience or activity. Then you have to *retain* it—that is, hold it steady in your mind and keep it from disappearing. Then you have to *inspect* it—study it and make inferences about it. Finally, you have to be able to *transform* it—alter it in some way to suit your higher purposes.

Some people are good at some of these but not all four. They can generate an idea, but they can't hold on to it or transform it. My problem was that I was generating a lot of ideas, but generating was at odds with my need to retain, inspect, and transform. That's when I discovered the video camera, which is the technical heart of much of my scratching. When I improvise in a studio, alone or with other dancers, I always have a video camera getting everything on tape, so I can review it later. For me, scratching for ideas became a technical scheme of improvising (generating ideas), getting them on tape (retaining), watching the tapes later on (inspecting), and finding a way to use them in a dance (transforming).

There are as many ways to scratch for ideas as there are ideas:

The most common is **reading**. If you're like me, reading is your first line of defense against an empty head. It's how you learned as a child. It's how you absorb difficult information. It's how you keep your mind disciplined. If you monitor your reading assiduously, it's even how you grade your brain's conditioning; like an athlete in training, the more you read, the more mentally fit you feel. It doesn't matter if it's a book, magazine, newspaper, billboard, instruction manual, or cereal box—reading generates ideas, because you're literally filling your head with ideas and letting your imagination filter them for something useful. If I stopped reading, I'd stop thinking. It's that simple.

For a certain type of artist, particularly storytellers and songwriters, everyday conversation is scratching. If you listen, you will hear ideas. I always liked Paul McCartney's explanation of how he and John Lennon wrote "Eight Days a Week." McCartney was in a chauffeur-driven car on his way to Lennon's suburban home to work with him. He asked the driver, "How've you been?" "Working hard," said the driver, "working eight days a week." McCartney had never heard the phrase before and mentioned it to Lennon as they sat down to work. "Right," said Lennon, and instantly launched into "Ooh, I need your lovin' . . ." They wrote the song on the spot.

You can scratch for ideas by enjoying other people's handiwork, whether it's in a museum or a theater or an exhibition. When his operettas began to lose the public's favor, W. S. Gilbert, the wordsmithing half of Gilbert and Sullivan, grew desperate for a bold reinvention of the form—or at least a good idea. He got it by attending a London exhibition of Japanese culture. This gave Gilbert the idea for *The Mikado*, inspired his partner Arthur Sullivan to compose his greatest score, and linked into a wave of Japanophilia rolling through Europe. All because of a visit to an exhibition.

You can also scratch in the footsteps of your mentors and heroes, using their paradigms as a starting point for ideas. But you have to be careful. When I was beginning, I would sometimes find myself solving problems in exactly the same way that teachers such as Martha Graham and Merce Cunningham solved them. I would catch myself and say, "Wait a minute. That's how Martha or Merce would do it. We can't have that." Scratching among the paradigms is a dangerous habit if it turns you into an imitator rather than a creator.

You can scratch amid **nature**. Mozart and Beethoven, for example, were ardent bird lovers. They would get musical motifs from listening to birds. Bird songs don't do the same for me. I would have to see a bird move—how it waddles, how it stays close to its center, how it flies—to spark an idea. But an actor might get an idea about character by studying the carriage of a bird. A painter would study the bird's coloring.

Reading, conversation, environment, culture, heroes, mentors, nature—all are lottery tickets for creativity. Scratch away at them and you'll find out how big a prize you've won.

The tricky part about scratching, however, is that you can't stop with one idea. Henry James said that genius is the act of perceiving similarity among disparate things. In the empty room you're trying to connect the dots, linking A to B to C to maybe come up with H. Scratching is a means to identifying A, and if you can get to A, you've got a grip on the slippery rock wall. You've got purchase. You can move on to B, which is mandatory. You cannot stop with one idea. You don't really have a workable idea until you combine two ideas.

It's a simple dynamic. If you want to see it dramatized, watch Mike Nichols's 1988 film *Working Girl*. It is ostensibly a Manhattan fairy tale about a lower-middle-class woman (played by Melanie Griffith) trying to climb out of the secretarial pool at an investment bank and win her prince charming (Harrison Ford). But it's infinitely more interesting if you see it as a movie about creativity. This "working girl" knows how to scratch. She gets ideas everywhere. She reads a gossip item about a radio disc jockey. She also sees a business magazine piece about a conglomerate on the prowl for acquisitions, and an item about its founder's daughter getting married. She puts the ideas together and tries to broker a deal for the conglomerate to acquire a radio network. At the end, she's challenged to describe how she came up with the plan for the acquisition. It's a telling scene. She has just been fired. On her way out of the building, with all her files and personal items packed in a box (a box just like mine!), she gets a chance to explain her thought process to the mogul:

> *See? This is* Forbes. *It's just your basic article about how you were looking to expand into broadcasting. Right? Okay now. The same day—I'll never forget this—I'm reading Page Six of the* New York Post *and there's this item on Bobby Stein, the radio talk show guy who does all those gross jokes about Ethiopia and the Betty Ford Center. Well, anyway, he's hosting this charity auction that night. Real bluebloods and won't that be funny? Now I turn the page to Suzy who does the society stuff and there's this picture of your daughter—see, nice picture—and she's helping to organize the charity ball. So I started to think: Trask, Radio, Trask, Radio. . . . So now here we are.*

He's impressed and hires her on the spot. Forget the fairy-tale plot; as a demonstration of how to link A to B and come up with C, *Working Girl* is a primer in the art of scratching.

Actually, in business it's perfectly legitimate to use the ideas you've scratched for without worrying about transforming them into something new. A talent agent I know was meeting with an opera singer to discuss ways to enlarge her career and broaden her appeal to the popular market. The diva mentioned that she would like to see some of the famous arias she'd recorded appear in films and on movie soundtracks, so millions of people would be exposed to her voice. A worthy objective. The executive had an idea for her: He showed her how the songwriter Burt Bacharach had produced a 4-CD limited edition of all the different singers who have recorded his hits over the years. He stamped out one thousand copies of this private anthology and sent them to music executives and producers around the world. Bacharach's objective was to get producers thinking of him when they were looking for tunes for their recording artists and soundtracks. The agent suggested the same for the diva: print up a private anthology of her best arias for the wider music community beyond the opera world. The agent was quite pleased with himself when he told me this useful idea. To my eye, he had taken A (Bacharach's idea) and B (the diva's desire to broaden her market) and come up with A (do the same as Bacharach). It was smart and practical, and it was probably the right answer. He'd done his homework. He hadn't done anything particularly creative, but then that wasn't his goal.

Now, don't get me wrong. I'm not knocking this sort of connective thinking in business. It's smart and practical. Use what worked before and adapt it to your situation. With profits, paychecks, and promotions at stake, it's only natural to try to reduce the risk by relying on what's already worked. We've all been in meetings to deal with a problem. Everyone is stumped until someone remembers how another group solved the same problem. Everyone nods with relief. "Great idea," says the boss. "Let's do that." And moves on. That's legitimate connective thinking in business.

But an artist cannot do that. People don't want to see you copying someone else (in fact, if you do, they take special delight in figuring out who or what you have copied). Art is not about minimizing risk and delivering work that is guaranteed to please. Artists have bigger goals. If being an artist means pushing the envelope, you don't want to stuff your material in someone else's envelope. You don't want to know the envelope has been invented. You want to find that out on your own.

Scratching is a wildly unruly process. But a few rules can make it a bit more manageable.

Be in Shape.

Scratching takes longer when you're rusty. Just as an athlete performs better if he's in top shape, ideas will come to you more quickly if you've been putting in the time at your chosen craft. If it's my first day back after a long layoff, I'm prepared to write off a whole week of work; I know much of it will be worthless, but I have to go through that process to get my mind and body back into shape. When my conditioning is right, I can feel productive in two or three minutes. You may already know this. Whatever your medium, if you've been away from it for a few weeks, the first days are going to be clumsy and fruitless. But things get easier as the rust falls away. The ideas come more smoothly. The hands on the instrument, the fingers at the keyboard, the eye at the easel respond in sync to the urgings of your mind and heart. You are fit and gleaming. You can't wait to attack your work.

Scratch in the Best Places.

When I'm searching for music for a dance, I go immediately to the best composers: Mozart, Beethoven, Brahms, Haydn. I listen to all their music because I want to educate my ear and, more important, I want to find their best music. You only go around once in this life, so I'm not interested in creating dances to their minor works.

I'm ruthless about this. I look at scratching in the best places as if I were working at a tailor's table. You've got the bolt of fabric, the tracing paper patterns, the pins to attach the pattern to the fabric, the scissors to cut the fabric, and the thread to stitch it all together. But the key is the fabric. The better the fabric, the more likely you will do your best work. That's why finding a great piece of music is key to making a great dance. The better the music, the better the dance. My objective is not to screw it up.

Sculptors know that half their job is selecting the best stone to work with. It's all in the material. If they get the best material, they are over the hump. Directors say the same thing about casting: If you've got the best people, it's hard to go wrong. That's the way I feel about scratching among the masters. It makes it so much easier to get home.

You should do the same. If you read for inspiration, read the top-drawer writers, and read their masterworks first. If you get your inspiration from art, look at the masters. If it's movies, focus on directors in the pantheon of greats. Scratch among the best and you will automatically raise the quality of ideas you uncover.

Never Scratch the Same Place Twice.

An integral part of Ulysses S. Grant's battle strategy was to never go back over the same terrain—you might meet the enemy pursuing you. More important, you gain no new information if you retrace your steps over already familiar land. Grant was always scouting new routes over new ground. That works for me, too, with scratching. I improvise in new rooms, turn on different music, change my reading habits, all in an effort to fight off old habits and shake myself up. If you scratch the same way all the time, you'll end up in the same place with the same old ideas.

Maintain the White Hot Pitch.

You've been there when a boss throws a temper tantrum in a meeting. Everyone in the room goes "Uh oh! The boss is mad. We better shape up." The tantrum, judiciously applied, is a great wake-up call to get people to do something. It's the same for you when you're alone and scratching for an idea. Throw a tantrum at yourself. Anger is a cheap adrenaline rush, but when you're going nowhere and can't get started, it will do.

Scratching is not about control and repose. It's about unleashing furious mindless energy and watching it bounce off everything in your path. The hope is that a spark will fly from all that contact and combustion—and it usually does.

I liken this mindless high-energy state to lifting deadweight off the ground. There is a moment when you've bent your knees, grabbed the bar, and are about to neutralize the massive gravity of this object. At that moment your mind is blank. You are all impulse and intention. You cannot think about the weight. You just have to lift it.

It's the same with scratching. When you're scratching for an idea, you don't need to think ahead. You have to trust the unconscious rush and let it hurtle forward unedited and unencumbered. Let it be awful and awkward and wrong. You can fix the results later, but you won't generate the ideas at all if you cool down the white hot pitch.

Scratching is where creativity begins. It is the moment where your ideas first take flight and begin to defy gravity. If you try to rein it in, you'll never know how high you can go.

exercises

11 Chaos and Coins

Gathering chaos into a satisfying order is a daunting challenge. You have to train for this struggle. Here is my favorite exercise.

I take a handful of coins. It doesn't matter how many or what denomination. I toss them onto my worktable and study the result. Sometimes the coins fall into a random pattern that's pleasing. But not often. So I fiddle with the coins, moving them around into strange or familiar geometries. Along the way I'll line them up, stack them, tease them into shapes—a stolid cross perhaps or a fanciful Ursa Major star grouping. Eventually, I land on an arrangement that feels like a musical chord resolving. I look at the coins and they cry out, "This is us." There in a nutshell is the essence of creativity: There are a number of possibilities, but only one solution looks *inevitable.*

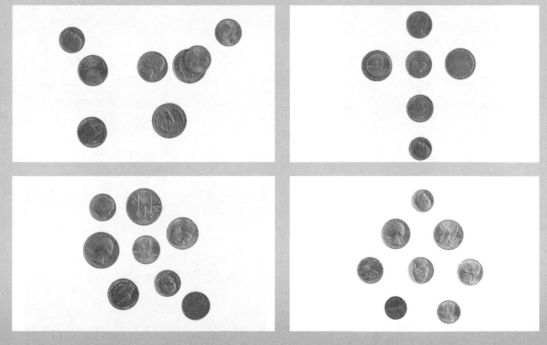

You can do this at home with poker chips, pickup sticks, paper clips—any everyday item that fits into your hand and can be easily tossed onto a desk and arranged into a harmonious pattern. I work with coins because they're readily at hand and shuffling them around is a nifty approximation of the arranging and rearranging of bodies I do in the studio. But even if the coins didn't correspond to dancers—if, for example, I was a painter or composer—I'd still find this a useful mental warm-up. Just as athletes prepare their bodies to *want* to work, so this exercise can help you feel more optimistic about resolving disorder. Once I feel that, I put the coins away. I have already begun.

12 Reading Archaeologically

I read for a lot of reasons, pleasure being the least of them.

I read *competitively,* remembering Mark Twain's admonition that "the man who does not read has no advantage over the man who cannot read."

I read for *growth,* firmly believing that what you are today and what you will be in five years depends on two things: the people you meet and the books you read.

Mostly, I read for *inspiration.* But what inspires me is probably not the same as what inspires or pleases the general populace. Although I'm interested in characters and story line and sheer information, I usually read with a specific purpose: I'm searching for patterns and archetypes, concepts and situations that are so basic to the human condition that they'll connect with an audience in a fundamental way, whether or not the audience is aware of the connection.

I tend to read "archaeologically." Meaning, I read backwards in time. I'll start with a contemporary book and then move on to a text that predates that book, and so on until I'm reading the most ancient texts and the most primitive ideas. For example, when I was casting about for the project that ultimately became the *Bacchae* piece, which is described in Chapter 7, I began by reading Nietzsche's *The Birth of Tragedy.* That hooked me on Dionysus, and led me back to Carl Kerenyi's study of *Dionysos,* which explained the place of goats as part of the worship of Dionysus, and the connection to the development of Greek tragedy. From there it was back to Euripides, and the text of *The Bacchae,* at last turning to a source that Jerome Robbins had suggested to me years earlier.

I don't know if many people read archaeologically. A lot of people I know read chronologically: If they're tackling all of Dostoyevsky, they start with his earliest works and plow through to his last writings, in much the same fashion as they did in school. Nothing wrong with that. They want to read along as the author grows from youth to maturity.

I do it the other way, as if I'm conducting a dig. I start with where the author ended and finish where he started. I've done this with Melville and Balzac as well as Dostoyevsky—and each time I feel like a detective solving the mystery of how the writer got that way, not how the writer ended up. A story told backwards is just as interesting as a story told the traditional way, maybe more so. The surest method for finding the path through a maze is to start at the end and work your way back to the beginning.

When I'm reading archaeologically, I'm not reading for pleasure. I read the way I scratch for an idea, digging down deep so I can get something out of it and use it in my work. I read *transactionally:* How can I use this? It's not enough for me to read a book. I have to "own" it. I scribble in the margins. I circle sentences I like and connect them with arrows to other useful sentences. I draw stars and exclamation points on every good page, to the point where the book is almost unreadable. By writing all over the pages, I transform the author's work into my book—and mine alone. (I hope, dear reader, you've been doing the same to this text throughout.)

Conduct your own reading dig. Take an author or a subject and start with the most recent text. Then work your way backwards to progressively older texts. If it's a novelist's body of work, you'll learn just as much about the author's recurring themes, philosophy, and style—but trust me, you'll see them from an entirely different point of view. If it's a particular subject, go back to the writer's original sources; the distance you've traveled with the writer and how the idea has changed will intrigue you. But you will get something more precious as well: the original idea in its ancient and most unadulterated form.

P.S.: I have two other reading habits: I "read fat," and I'm addicted to the *Oxford English Dictionary.*

"Reading fat" means not only reading, say, a novel, but reading related texts surrounding the novel, which may be books by the writer's contemporaries, or commentaries on the novel, or a biography of the writer, or the writer's letters. I admit it's a compulsive way to read, but you mine more out of every book. You can listen fat and see fat, too. If I'm listening to a Mozart quintet, I don't appreciate the piece as well as I do when I also listen to the works Mozart composed immediately before and after it. Likewise, with a painting, I like to see what the artist produced before and after the work at hand.

As for the *OED,* digging into the source of a word's meaning is a great way to scratch for core ideas. Nothing in the English language fascinates me more than the multitude of definitions for words I think I know. Consulting the *OED* sitting on its table in my work area reminds me that I only know a fraction of what I think I know. Before I write about an idea such as *ritual,* I'll look it up in the *OED.* But it's not enough to digest the word's sixteen definitions. Reading fat means I also look up the words immediately before and after "ritual." You never know. The next good idea may be hiding there.

13 A Dozen Eggs

The exercise I call Egg is a great way to start a creative session. It couldn't be simpler: I sit on the floor, bring my knees to my chest, curl my head down to my knees, and try to make myself as small as I can. In this minimalized shrunken state, I have nowhere else to go; I cannot become smaller, I can only expand and grow. And so it becomes a ritual of discovery for me. If I lift my head and straighten my back I become Tall Egg. If I stretch out my legs and point my toes, forming an L-shape, I become Jackknife Egg. I stick with it as long as it remains interesting, sometimes going through as many as a hundred positions. I've been doing this daily for years and I usually find something new in the process. I remember one time sitting in a ball and twisting slightly so I inched forward. Eureka! I discovered Walking

Egg, which led to Walking Backwards Egg and a dozen other new positions. I live for those moments. The discovery delights me and lifts my spirit—and keeps me coming back to Egg.

Naming the positions is optional, a mental game that I consider a perk of the job.

I like the Egg routine because it is so basic. You don't need to know anything or be in particularly good shape to do it (although some stretching is a definite help). The only requirement is a commitment to the process. The starting Egg position is your home base and you are setting out to see how far you can travel from home.

It may remind you of yoga, but there's a difference. In yoga (or any other prescribed exercise routine) you are following a defined sequence of poses and positions that are good for different parts of the body. That's not what's going on here. There's no instructor or manual telling you what to do, no exact purpose to the movements. You're not asking anyone "What do I do next?" You're following your impulses, letting your mind and body provide you with the answers.

I also like Egg because it forces you to think about change. Once you shrink yourself into a fetal ball, you have no choice but to do something expansive. You cannot hold the starting position forever, though you can hold it for as long as you like. Eventually, though, you'll have to do something. Egg is an exercise that teaches you how to accomplish the most difficult task in any creative endeavor: *begin.*

Egg makes you move. I can't say enough about the connection between body and mind; when you stimulate your body, your brain comes alive in ways you can't simulate in a sedentary position. The brain is an organ, tied integrally to all the other systems in the body, and it's affected by blood flow, neural transmission, all the processes you undergo when you put your body through its paces. You're making it work differently, and new directions can result. I recommend you keep a pad and pencil nearby while doing Egg for fresh ideas. You probably already know that when you're frustrated with your efforts, it helps to get up and walk around the room. Egg takes the principle and channels it without the frustration.

Finally, it imparts a lesson about skill. You don't have to be a gymnast or dancer to get something out of Egg, but it helps. The more conditioning you bring to it, the farther you can go. I'm a trained dancer. I am accustomed to the tortures and contortions the body can endure, and I feel that I've seen nearly everything the body can do. Yet when I introduce Egg at colleges, the students often come up with Egg positions that are new to me. Their fearless young minds and bodies have come up with such novelties as Exploded Egg, Scrambled Egg, Humpty-Dumpty, Egg on the Half-Shell, Runny Egg, Egg-Cited, and Eggs-Aspirated.

Egg will take you places you've never been. Make it a part of your daily routine.

14 Give Yourself a Little Challenge

George Harrison once decided, as a game, to write a song based on the first book he saw at his mother's house. Picking one up at random, he opened it and saw the phrase "gently weeps," whereupon he promptly wrote his first great song, "While My Guitar Gently Weeps."

You can give yourself the same kind of challenge whatever medium you work in: paint only in shades of green; write a story without using the verb "to be"; film a ten-minute scene nonstop with one camera. Giving yourself a handicap to overcome will force you to think in a new and slightly different way, which is the prime goal of scratching.

15 Take a Field Trip

When scratching turns into frustration, take a walk. But don't just walk anywhere. Add some utility to it. Have a goal. Turn it into a field trip by imbuing the walk with a steely determination to come back with something in hand.

If I'm struggling for an idea, I often find myself leaving my studio, walking across Central Park, and ending up at the Metropolitan Museum of Art. Museums are my favorite field trips, and working in museum-rich Manhattan, I would be a fool to ignore the local resources. As Goethe said, "He who cannot draw on three thousand years is living from hand to mouth." But it's easy to lose yourself and exhaust yourself in a resource as rich as the Met. So you ought to go with a goal. Attack the museum with a purpose.

For example, dancers see themselves in a mirror since their first day in a dance studio, and that is often the only way they perceive themselves. I want them to realize new ways of presenting the human body. This is particularly true with dancers new to my company and my work. So I take them to the Met to share some sources that inspired me—and may do the same for them.

On one trip to the Met I started with the three-thousand-year-old Cycladic figures, the paper-thin sculptures whose crossed-arm position became the closing image of *The Fugue.* Then it was off to the African wing where the wooden fertility statues, with their bottom-heavy proportions, hunkering low to the ground, suggest the squatting in my 1998 dance *Yemaya.* Finally we moved to the Egyptian wing to look at an array of striding figures, all locked into the isometric tension that my fierce warriors would need for *In the Upper Room.* And then, with our minds opened but not overloaded, we were done.

In this spirit, the whole world becomes a museum that you can own.

Professional musicians are also huge beneficiaries of the world's secret resources. They are always traveling to perform and, for them, music is a universal language. If they have ears, a visit to any new musical culture becomes a field trip. Thus, Antonín Dvořák visits Iowa in 1887 and the result is his Ninth Symphony, *From the New World,* his most famous composition. Jazz pianist Dave Brubeck tours the Middle East and India in 1958 where he becomes intrigued by folk music that doesn't stick to 4/4 time and the result is his enormous commercial breakthrough, the 1959 album *Time Out,* with hits like "Take Five" in 5/4 meter and "Blue Rondo a la Turk" in 9/8 time. Paul Simon hears recordings of South African street music in 1984, visits South Africa in 1985, and the result a year later is his much-admired record *Graceland*.

It doesn't matter where you live. If you have a goal in mind, you can turn any venue or destination into a valuable field trip. If you're looking for beauty and sensory relief, it could be a local gallery or a walk in the woods. If you want chaos and exposed human emotions, spend some time in a hospital emergency room or a bus terminal. If you want information, pore over documents in a forgotten archive at your library. If you want to observe people under pressure, check out a police station or loiter around a construction site. A mall, a blues club, a dairy farm, an open field—they are all worthwhile field trips if you have a clear purpose in mind. It's your world. Own it.

Chapter 7

accidents will happen

The most productive artists I know have a plan in mind when they get down to work. They know what they want to accomplish, how to do it, and what to do if the process falls off track.

But there's a fine line between good planning and overplanning. You never want the planning to inhibit the natural evolution of your work.

The photographer Richard Avedon is as good at planning and preparation as anyone I know. Before he takes a portrait of a subject, he knows exactly what kind of camera, film, props, and background he will use. Everything is planned ahead. None of his technique is left to chance. Unlike many portrait photographers, Avedon takes preparation a step further and insists on meeting the subjects before the photo session. But all that planning ends at the moment the subject walks into the studio; that's when instinct and creativity take over. Avedon doesn't have a preconceived notion of what he wants the photo to look like, though he does know what feeling it should convey. He plans ahead, but not too far ahead, so he can recognize *amazing* when he sees it. When he photographed Charlie Chaplin, it was the very day the great comedian was leaving America. He was annoyed and it showed. He stubbornly refused to give Avedon any emotion other than a blank stare. But then there was a split-second moment when Chaplin's theatrical instincts slipped through. Chaplin pointed his index fingers above his head, creating horns, and, with his scowl, became an angry devil. Avedon believed that a portrait of Chaplin had to have the feel of humor. Equally stubborn and determined, he worked on breaking Chaplin's sullen mood. When Chaplin let his guard down, pretending to be a laughing devil with horns, Avedon snapped. End of photo session. He got what he wanted.

A plan is like the scaffolding around a building. When you're putting up the exterior shell, the scaffolding is vital. But once the shell is in place and you start work on the interior, the scaffolding disappears. That's how I think of planning. It has to be sufficiently thoughtful and solid to get the work up and standing straight, but it cannot take over as you toil away on the interior guts of a piece. Transforming your ideas rarely goes according to plan.

This, to me, is the most interesting paradox of creativity: In order to be habitually creative, you have to know how to prepare to be creative, but good planning alone won't make your efforts successful; it's only after you let go of your plans that you can breathe life into your efforts.

When I was making *Surfer at the River Styx,* I had trouble coming up with an ending. I was yearning for something majestic and I wasn't getting it. Then, one day in rehearsal, I saw it. I wanted all four men in the company on stage near the end of the ballet, and I had them partnering one of the women. Four men, one woman. This is not usually done. Perhaps something unusual can happen with that combination. They were holding her low off the ground, and as she was circling around their arms and bodies in a very risky form of aerial partnering, I could see her gradually but organically snaking her way up their bodies. She just kept evolving and moving higher as the group of four men walked slowly toward the right side of the stage. And then it hit me: Omigod, what if they lifted her as high as possible, holding her legs in a perfect split? Lit properly (that is, theatrically), she'd be floating in air. That's the ending!

It was a stroke of luck, but I was prepared to accept it for the simple reason that I needed an ending. At that moment I felt blessed, because it sent the piece into a sphere where the entire dance was suddenly coherent. I certainly hadn't planned it. It was a gift. But I also felt I'd earned it.

Your creative endeavors can never be thoroughly mapped out ahead of time. You have to allow for the suddenly altered landscape, the change in plan, the accidental spark—and you have to see it as a stroke of luck rather than a disturbance of your perfect scheme. Habitually creative people are, in E. B. White's phrase, "prepared to be lucky."

The key words here are "prepared" and "lucky." They're inseparable. You don't get lucky without preparation, and there's no sense in being prepared if you're not open to the possibility of a glorious accident. The sports entrepreneur Mark McCormack, whose career began with three enormous consecutive strokes of luck—golf legends Arnold Palmer, Gary Player, and Jack Nicklaus were his first three clients—once said, "Yes, I admit I was lucky. But I saw it and I was ready for it, whereas many people wouldn't know a stroke of luck if it bit them on the nose."

Some people resent the idea of luck. Accepting the role of chance in our lives suggests that our creations and triumphs are not entirely our own, and that in some way we're undeserving of our success. I say, Get over it. This is how the world works. In creative endeavors luck is a skill.

The discovery of vulcanized rubber is the perfect example of the power of luck. Charles Goodyear, after years of experimentation, walks into a general store in 1839, accidentally spills his concoction of gum and sulphur onto a sizzling potbelly stove, and discovers that instead of melting like molasses the compound chars like leather, leaving a dry, springy material that keeps its flexibility at almost any temperature. Goodyear called the process "vulcanization" and almost every use of rubber depends on it. It is one of the most celebrated "accidents" in industrial science. Goodyear, of course, didn't see it that way, and I side with Goodyear. He was active in his pursuit of a durable rubber, not passive; he was always experimenting and therefore always open to luck. Also, while the accident could have happened to anybody at any time, it took a person with an open mind to recognize the importance of what took place on that stove, and it took knowledge and skill to analyze it and repeat it in the laboratory. The hot stove incident held meaning, said Goodyear, only for the person "whose mind was prepared to draw an inference," the one who had "applied himself most perseveringly to the subject." (Gary Player put this principle succinctly: "The more I practice, the luckier I get.")

Being prepared for luck is like getting a voice message that tells you, "Something good may happen to you between 9:00 A.M. and 5:00 P.M. today. Make sure you're at your desk (or in your studio or office or at your laboratory bench) working. And keep your eyes open for it."

Of course, you have to be present, in the room, to recognize the stroke of luck. Being in the room is a concomitant of Goodyear's perseverance: The more you are in the room working, experimenting, banging away at your objective, the more luck has a chance of biting you on the nose.

Woody Allen said that eighty percent of success in show business is showing up. It's the same with luck: eighty percent of it is showing up to see it. My dancers can be doing the most marvelous things in the studio, but if I'm not there to witness it, it may as well be the proverbial tree falling in the forest. Never happened.

Advertising wizard Phil Dusenberry established his career as a creative director by landing the General Electric account. GE was looking to consolidate all its advertising at one shop and they wanted a corporate slogan that unified the message. On the day before his presentation to the GE executives, Dusenberry didn't feel the slogan was quite right. He had the concept—"We make the things that make life good . . ." or something like that—but he didn't feel it gelled. So he laid out the various slogans and started rearranging the words, in much the same fashion as I play with my coins. Eventually the words fell into place and spelled out "We bring good things to life." Dusenberry knew this was the winner the moment he saw it. Was this luck or accident? Would anyone else have recognized the perfect slogan? Would anyone else have bothered to play with the words? Dusenberry was prepared, he was persevering in the room, and he was able to see it.

It's tempting to try to rein in the unruliness of the creative process, especially at the start. Planning lets you impose order on the chaotic process of making something new, but when it's taken too far you get locked into a status quo, and creative thinking is about breaking free from the status quo, even from one you made yourself. That's why it's vital to know the difference between good planning and too much planning.

Over the years I've learned a thing or two—entirely the hard way—about the pitfalls of locking yourself into a predetermined course. I started out in the not-for-profit world of dance, where much of my sustenance came from foundation grants. I became adept at writing grant applications that required me to specify exactly what I intended to do with the grant money—from the music I would commission or license to whom I'd hire to design the costumes. No detail was left to chance. As a result, I fell into the habit of overplanning. Since I like to keep my promises, I developed a stoic reluctance to change. My focus on preparation and ritual made it difficult for me to veer away from my plan.

But working in real time in the real world eventually showed me the error of my ways. I began to see that overplanning can be as pernicious as not planning at all. There's an emotional lie to overplanning; it creates a security blanket that lets you assume you have things under control, that you are further along than you really are, that you're home free when you haven't even walked out the door yet.

When I was first considering writing this book, I thought about calling it *How Not to Plan.* That title appealed to the contrarian in me. I wanted people to take note that planning isn't everything, that being too organized can be a negative. It hems you into a corner, handcuffs you, and as a result, shortchanges your opportunities to be lucky. To embrace luck, you have to enhance your tolerance for ambiguity. *Plan only to a point.* The great military strategists from Sun-tzu to Clausewitz have advised that you can plan only so far into the battle; you have to save lots of room for your adversary's contribution.

Let's take a look at some of the problems that can derail your well-laid plans.

Other People.

When I prepare to work on a project, the field general in me comes out immediately. I marshal all my forces. I carefully assemble my team, from dancers to technical support. Anything less would be underplanning.

But people sometimes let you down. For every person who inspires you and pushes you in the right direction, there is often another who is "missing in action," either because he's unreliable or simply closes you off rather than opens you up. No matter how well-intentioned someone else may be, things go wrong—dancers get injured, a loved one is taken ill, someone hits a creative roadblock just as you're breaking through your own—and you have to be able to roll with the changes and work with them instead of resisting. The peg may have started out round but it's square now; hammering harder isn't going to make it fit.

Relying too much on others, even in an inevitably collaborative process, makes you lazy. Don't get me wrong, I love the people I work with. Unlike the solitary painter or writer, I do nothing but collaborations; it's not me up there onstage dancing anymore. The dancers are my collaborators, as are the composer, the musicians, and the costume, set, and lighting designers. There is no one in the world more delighted than I when my production wizard Santo Loquasto, with whom I have worked for decades, strolls in with a set design that blows everyone away. But I can't ever let myself think, "Well, this section of the ballet is subpar. Thank God Santo's set design will save me here."

To protect himself against depending too much on movie stars, the film director Milos Forman has a style that keeps many actors on edge. He won't show them the script too far in advance. He won't rehearse them. He won't permit them to launch into their arias. He just starts the cameras rolling and tells them to say their lines. Actors hate that; they feel unprepared, under someone else's control. Which they are. It's the director's duty to let nothing interfere with the telling of the story, and in Forman's view that includes the actors. He is the one with responsibility for the Big Picture, a perspective he has to maintain at all times no matter what the priorities might be for the performer on that day's set. (On the other hand, they have to admit it works: three actors have won Academy Awards in his films. Forman's efforts make his actors lucky.)

Perfectionism at the Start.

Another trap is the belief that everything has to be perfect before you can take the next step. You won't move on to that second chapter until the first is written, rewritten, honed, tweaked, examined under a microscope, and buffed to a bright mahogany sheen. You won't dip a brush in the paint until you've assembled all the colors you can possibly imagine using in the course of the project. I know it's important to be prepared, but at the start of the process this type of perfectionism is more like procrastination. You've got to get in there and *do*.

I used to bask in the notion that all my obstacles to creative efficiency would vanish if I only had exactly the right resources: my own studio, my own dancers, my own theater, and enough money to pay the dancers all year long and to hire the best collaborators. But I've learned that the opposite is true: Limits are a secret blessing, and bounty can be a curse. I've been on enough big-budget film sets to appreciate the malignant influence of abundance and bloat.

A good manager in business knows that there's never a moment in the business cycle when a company's objectives and resources are in perfect harmony. There's never an ideal balance between how many orders you have and how much inventory you're stocking. Your expenses and your income are never exactly in sync; one is always outpacing the other. Your people always demand more money, more resources, more investment spending than you're willing to give; you always have more phone calls to return or paperwork to handle than time to get it all done. Good managers know this instinctively, so they never plan on an ideal harmony they can't achieve. It's better to be ready to go than to wait until you are perfectly ready.

For my first dance, the seven-minute-long *Tank Dive* performed in Room 1604 at Hunter College in New York City in 1965, I had no money, no scenery, no music, no stage to speak of. How limited is that? In fact, for my first five years I choreographed to silence. And yet those impoverished circumstances forced me to discover my own dance vocabulary. Dizzy Gillespie once said of Louis Armstrong's giant influence on jazz, "No him, no me." I feel the same way about my years of extremely limited resources: No deprivation, no inspiration. No then, no now.

Even George Balanchine, who created a blissful cocoon of nearly unlimited resources at New York City Ballet, liked to feel that he worked under restrictions. When someone asked him how he made dances, he replied, "On union time." Meaning, he could only create when he had the dancers in the room, and the dancers were in the room for only fifty-five minutes at a time, between their union-mandated hourly five-minute breaks. Balanchine had everything a choreographer needed—his own company, his own theater, his own orchestra (!), his own deep-pocketed patrons—yet even he had limits imposed: He operated at the mercy of AGMA, the dancers' union. Based on the evidence, he obviously made it work.

Remember this the next time you moan about the hand you're dealt: No matter how limited your resources, they're enough to get you started. Time, for example, is our most limited resource, but it is not the enemy of creativity that we think it is. The ticking clock is our friend if it gets us moving with urgency and passion. Give me a writer who thinks he has all the time in the world and I'll show you a writer who never delivers. Likewise with money, which comes a close second as our most limited resource. It's tempting to believe that the quantity and quality of our creative productivity would increase exponentially if only we could afford everything we've imagined, but I've seen too many artists dry up the moment they had enough money in the bank. For every artist who is empowered and inspired by money, there is another who gets lazy and self-satisfied because of it. Necessity will continue to be the mother of invention.

The Wrong Structure.

Creating is all about playing and innovating within familiar forms. It's natural to want to establish as many ground rules as possible about form before we get down to work, but you have to choose the form that's not only appropriate to you but right for your particular idea.

The novel that seems to be going nowhere might be better as a short story; conversely, the story whose characters are bursting with unfulfilled promise should grow into a novella. The screenplay whose dialogue crackles but lacks a strong visual component could make a great one-act play. The portrait whose lines fascinate but in which color is a distraction might have a sculpture inside it dying to come out.

Poets face this all the time because of the multitude of forms. Free verse liberates, but haiku concentrates. Poems come in many forms, from sonnets to villanelles to pantoums and sestinas. Some forms confine the poet, others make him or her sing.

The sestina, for example, is a puzzling form, handed down from the twelfth-century French troubadour Arnaut Daniel. It consists of thirty-nine lines—six stanzas of six lines each with an envoi of three lines at the end. It does not rhyme. Instead, the lines must end with just six different words throughout, and there is a prescribed pattern for these repetitions: The word that appears at the end of a stanza must end the first line of the next stanza, and the end-word of the first line of each stanza moves to the second line of the next stanza. It's amazing that such a goofily willful form survives, but some contemporary poets are intrigued by all that self-guiding structure. W. H. Auden tried his hand at one sestina; it's called *"Paysage Moralisé,"* and you can find it in his *Collected Poems.* It acquires a certain power through its numbing repetitions, but it strikes me as more of a parlor trick than a deeply felt poem.

The sonnet has a very clear structure requiring fourteen lines of iambic pentameter with a defined rhyme scheme, but it is still flexible enough to breathe. You can select from the three major rhyme schemes: Italian, Spenserian, and Shakespearean. Unlike the testy sestina, the sonnet's length and rhymes make it pleasing to the ear, and provide room for linguistic and thematic invention. You need look no further than Shakespeare's 154 sonnets for proof of the beauty and range possible within the confines of the sonnet. The difference between the sonnet and the sestina is the difference between going fishing with a fishing net or in a diving bell: Both devices are built for the water, but the diving bell is hard, inviolate, confining, and inviting only to extremely curious fish; the net is flexible, porous, and expansive—perfectly designed to haul 'em in.

A Sense of Obligation.

I once spent six weeks rehearsing sixteen dancers on a bad piece of music called "The Hollywood Kiss" because I felt obligated to a composer who had done a favor for me. I had a company of dancers on full payroll, so I was obliged to keep them busy. I was obligated to the studio I had rented out and the staff I had hired. But obligation, I eventually saw, is not the same as commitment, and it's certainly not an acceptable reason to stick with something that isn't working. So, after six weeks of going nowhere with the meter running, I scuttled the project. Despite the most meticulous planning—or more likely because of it—I wasted six weeks of everyone's time. In hindsight, I should have heeded the CEO who told me, "You only need one good reason to commit to an idea, not four hundred. But if you have four hundred reasons to say yes and one reason to say no, the answer is probably no."

Whatever your reasons for starting with a project—whether crass or noble—they have to be clear and unencumbered. Obligation is a flimsy base for creativity, way down the list behind passion, courage, instinct, and the desire to do something great.

The Wrong Materials.

Another error of planning is to pursue a goal with the wrong materials. I used to be guilty of this. I'd be hell-bent on making a quartet, and only three dancers would show up at rehearsal that day. I would fume to myself, "It's not fair!" I was so locked into my plan for four dancers that I'd be totally unprepared to work with three. An entire day would be lost. Eventually I wised up and saw the flaw in any method of working that doesn't accommodate the notion of injury to dancers. Injuries are part of the business. It's like a wedding planner not taking into consideration the possibility that an outdoor wedding reception might be sabotaged by rain. Solution: You put up a tent!

It took me a while to accept this. I tend toward optimism and ignore Murphy's Law ("Anything that can go wrong will") at every turn. But I learned to adapt and to plan differently. If you're fixated on making a quartet, I told myself, you'd better have four dancers and at least two understudies, because somebody will get injured and disappear for a spell, or else you shouldn't be making quartets.

These mistakes—relying too much on others, waiting for the perfect setup, king structure, feeling obligated to finish what you've started, and work-the wrong materials—are deadly. Any one of them will undermine your ts.

128

Incredibly, in what I like to think of as my sage years when I should have known better, I made all of these mistakes at once. It was in 1999, when the New York City Ballet, home of the Balanchine tradition, invited me to make a dance for the company.

I should have been on red alert the moment Peter Martins, the artistic director, generously put the entire company at my disposal. "It's all yours for the next four weeks," he said. "You can have any dancer you want. All the rehearsal time you need. Whatever musicians you want."

Whom the gods wish to destroy, they give unlimited resources.

With the extraordinary dancers of the City Ballet available to me, I turned to a musical selection I'd always loved, a late Beethoven piano sonata, #31 in A flat major, Op. 110. This might not have been my best impulse. After all, I had an entire world-class orchestra at my disposal, willing and able to play anything in the vast Western repertory. Instead, I said, "No thank you, I don't want an orchestra; I'll take one lonely piano player." Traditionally, City Ballet's dancers have "quiet feet"—that is, they don't make a lot of noise on the stage floor during a performance. This is very difficult to achieve, but it's characteristic of City Ballet training that their ballerinas practically float above the floor. I thought this would allow the sound of the solo piano to come through despite my desire to use a large complement of fourteen dancers. I had learned earlier from another Beethoven piano solo ballet that if you're using a great piece of music, the audience wants to hear it.

What makes NYCB special is not that it has some of the best dancers in the world, but that it has so many of them. I was like a kid in a toy store. I wanted to get every dancer I'd admired at NYCB into my ballet. I pushed some very accomplished soloists to dance in ensembles, which they considered demeaning. They all wanted to be featured, but I had a large cast and not everyone could get a satisfying star turn. Too many dancers, not enough notes. I would have been better off choreographing a duet.

Worse, the sound generated by so many feet, however well tempered, overwhelmed the music. As rehearsals progressed, I found myself asking them to be more and more quiet, to the point where it got to be a running joke. At night I had dreams of Balanchine up in heaven, chuckling down at me. "You silly woman," he said. "You're using Beethoven? I never used Beethoven. I was too smart to use Beethoven. He's too good and very tough to dance to. And why are you only using a piano? How many times have I told you, 'Use the damn orchestra!'? The audience has paid for it. They want to hear it. And it will make everything else bigger."

So two weeks into my four weeks of rehearsals it was out with the piano sonata and in with a really loud symphony that wouldn't be drowned out by dancing feet—in this case, Beethoven's jaunty, percussive Symphony #7.

Now I had to graft two weeks of choreography made to an intimate piano sonata onto that boisterous symphony. I could see that it wasn't working very well. Here is where the sense of obligation kicked in: I couldn't just throw out all the work we had done, because that would mean erasing two weeks of the entire company's time, which is worth a fortune. I felt obliged to the people providing me with these remarkable resources not to have wasted them.

I worked all night to make the changes fit the dancers, but then I ran into the human equation: While building a lot of the ballet on the wrong piece of music, I used up a big portion of the dancers' enthusiasm. Getting them re-excited midstream about a new piece of music created something of a credibility gap.

Moreover, I'd had to learn how the company functioned along the way. This was my first foray into the company on my own (I had co-choreographed *Brahms/Handel* with Jerome Robbins a decade earlier), and it slowly dawned on me that I was in the dark about a lot of things I normally take for granted. I didn't know how rehearsals were scheduled. I didn't know how the dancers behaved; they were in the midst of a season, rehearsing during the day while performing at night, and I didn't know their tolerance for new work or how much they would commit to such a project. I had to find that out as we went, and this added one more area of uncertainty and stress into the equation.

If that wasn't bad enough, I was mildly annoyed with the business deal that had brought me into City Ballet. Choreographers get a fee for their work, and I have worked long and hard to get one of the highest fees in the world. City Ballet doesn't play that way. Every choreographer gets the same fee, no matter who they are. It's called a Most Favored Nations clause. No one gets treated any better than anyone else, or any worse. I agreed to the deal but it must have bothered me subconsciously because my son, Jesse, picked up on it.

"Remind me, Jesse," I would ask him. "Why am I working so hard for so little money?"

"This is New York City Ballet," he would reply. "You're paying for the opportunity to hit a home run out of Yankee Stadium."

And I would go, "Yes, that's what I'm doing. I'm going to hit a home run out of Yankee Stadium."

That swing-for-the-fences mentality may be the most dangerous mistake I made. Everything I did was predicated on being bigger, bolder, grander. I was going to make a statement. I was going to change the company. All in one dance. At one point, in a display of hubris that makes me roar with laughter now, I actually asked the company to fly in the great Austrian conductor Carlos Kleiber (whose recording of Beethoven's Seventh I admired greatly) to conduct the premiere. And NYCB was so willing to cater to my whims (again, those unlimited resources!), they actually made some inquiries with the famously elusive conductor.

I could go on citing the petty misjudgments I made during this project, but you get the idea. When the ballet, called *The Beethoven Seventh,* premiered in January 2000, the response from audience and critics was respectful and in some cases quite warm. But it's not my favorite work or my best work, and I'll never be able to think about it without remembering the pains of the process. Considering that I went into the project hoping to make my mark in the annals of this historic company, I would have to say that I came up far short of my ambitions. This story could be taught at Harvard Business School as a case study: An executive gets a promotion to run a major division in a corporation, the company gives him a blank check to shake things up, and the new boss responds by (a) announcing unrealistic goals, (b) tackling the wrong problem out of the gate, (c) enlisting all the talented people he can find but assigning tasks that are not quite right for the people doing them, (d) changing his mind midstream, and (e) assuming he knows the only way to do things. A perfect plan for disaster.

Six weeks later I was across the Lincoln Center plaza at American Ballet Theatre to make a new ballet, my fifteenth for the company. The circumstances were ideally horrible. It was as if ABT management had decided to give me the opposite of City Ballet's carte blanche. ABT was giving me two weeks to mount a ballet from start to finish—an almost impossible schedule. The budget was minimal. Other than the two weeks, I had no fixed rehearsal times. If I wanted to use any of the principal dancers I would have to catch them on the run between other rehearsals and performances. The whole ballet would have to be spaced on stage, properly lit, and costumed in ninety minutes of technical rehearsal the afternoon of the world premiere. That day would also be the first time we would work with a live orchestra. Talk about limited resources!

In hindsight, it was an ideal situation for me. With a constricted timetable, bare-bones budget, and dancers I couldn't count on to be at my beck and call, I responded accordingly. The circumstances demanded total self-reliance and exquisite planning.

The process that resulted in the ballet *The Brahms-Haydn Variations* was, to my mind, a model of proper planning. After my recent City Ballet experience, I had no delusions of grandeur. I also knew my materials well, the dancers I would be using, and how much time I would have to rehearse. I made a virtue of the clock ticking (you can't overthink when you don't have time to think at all). I consider this piece the most satisfying ballet of my career.

The conditions were so limited that, as Samuel Johnson said about the prospect of being hanged, they concentrated the mind wonderfully.

exercises

16 Pick a Fight

Too much planning implies you've got it all under control. That's boring, unrealistic, and dangerous. It lulls you into a complacency that removes one of the artist's most valuable conditions: being pissed. Art is competitive with yourself, with the past, with the future. It is a special war zone where first you make the rules, and then you test the consequences.

Creativity is an act of *defiance.* You're challenging the status quo. You're questioning accepted truths and principles. You're asking three universal questions that mock conventional wisdom:

"Why do I have to obey the rules?"

"Why can't I be different?"

"Why can't I do it my way?"

These are the impulses that guide all creative people whether they admit it or not. Every act of creation is also an act of destruction or abandonment. Something has to be cast aside to make way for the new.

But those lofty goals are the farthest thing from your mind at the start of a project. In those moments, you need to channel your innate defiance productively. So, pick a fight—with the system, the rules, your rituals, even your everyday routines.

For one day, be completely contrary, to the point of orneriness and belligerence, with anything and everything you do. Turn everything upside down.

When you get up in the morning, pick a fight with your wake-up routine. If you like to exercise (as I do), do your workout in reverse, or twice as fast (whew!), or twice as slow (ugh!). The change will challenge your muscles. The discomfort will stimulate your brain.

When you set up to work, pick a fight with your rituals. Ask yourself why you need this ritual, what solace and protection does it bring, what state of mind does it create, what good does it produce. Questioning what's gone unquestioned gets the brain humming.

When you actually get down to work, pick a fight with your first impulse that day. Do the opposite of what your brain is telling you to do. That quick jolt of defiance might be enough to rewire your circuitry and deliver something new to your doorstep.

These are private exercises. You're picking a fight with yourself—to generate anger, emotion, combustion, and heat. You need to do this once in a while, if only to prepare yourself for the bigger battle, the one where you pick a fight with something outside yourself.

Sometimes the most creative thing you can do in business is to pick a fight with entrenched systems and hierarchies, if only to get people questioning the wisdom of doing things the same old way. I can't imagine any CEO taking over a company nowadays and telling his new subordinates, "Everything's fine. If it ain't broke, don't fix it." The smart CEOs come in swinging; they install their own team, establish new goals. In other words, they pick fights and start breaking things immediately.

Beethoven, the most truculent of artists, not only picked fights with musical forms, reinventing our notions of the shape and scope of symphonies and sonatas, he reinvented how society regarded composers and musicians. Before Beethoven, composers were treated like skilled servants; they were paid whatever their rich and royal patrons wanted to pay. Beethoven changed all that. He demanded and got lucrative fees for his services, and was one of the first composers to dine with his hosts rather than with the help when he performed in his patrons' homes. I don't think he could operate as an artist *without* the feeling that he was at war with someone or something.

This fighting mode is not for everyone, but there's something to be said for getting into a warrior's frame of mind, especially when you're troubled by some aspect of your creative life. If something isn't right in the piece you're working on, you can't always fix it by the sheer application of skill. Tinkering and tweaking will only take you so far. Sometimes, to force change, you have to attack the work with outrage and violence. You see this a lot of times with students who, in their work, pick fights with their teachers; instinctively, they sense they'll be judged on whom they do battle with. They know that in order to break away and find their own voice, they must defy, even mock, their artistic mentors.

You won't always win, but the exercise is liberating.

17 Our Perfect World

If I were sublimely fortunate, I would work in my perfect world daily. At rare times, I have been privileged to work with dancers on the following basis: I am exchanging my time for theirs, with no money or performance goals, no ulterior motive other than the mutual challenge in sight, just working together to create in an empty space. I call this uncomplicated condition Our Perfect World. These are my ground rules.

> Quiet.
> No one present who does not belong—no observers.
> All the time in the world. No worry that you will be thrown out or
> that you will go into overtime.
> No goal other than to try things.
> No fear of failure; nothing will fail.
> No obligations other than to do your best.
> We entertain each other: I challenge them, and they challenge me.
> Each day completes itself. The next day is new.

My perfect world does not exist, but it's there as a goal. What are the conditions of your perfect world? Which of them are essential, and which can you work around?

You may discover that you are not that far from heaven.

18 How to Be Lucky

Be *generous.*

I don't use that word lightly. Generosity is luck going in the opposite direction, away from you. If you're generous to someone, if you do something to help him out, you are in effect making him lucky. This is important. It's like inviting yourself into a community of good fortune.

Whenever I feel I'm working in a groove it's invariably because I feel I am being the benefactor in the situation rather than the beneficiary. I am sharing my art with others, lending my craft to theirs, interest-free with no IOU. I want the dancers to look great, so I try to give them great steps. In return, they live up to the potential I see in them. Then I am the one who feels lucky. In the luck equation, who is the winner here?

Someone once asked me why the superstar dancers of the ballet world don't make very good choreographers. The quick answer is that few of them have the facility to teach effectively since a lot of what they do has come so easily to them. But I think the bigger issue is generosity. Stars become stars because they have a gift for pulling the world into them; they draw people's attention through their beauty, talent, charisma, and wiles. As a result, I don't think they're generally willing to project their own artistic hopes and desires onto other people. They are used to having their own assets supported. This isn't evil selfishness or egotism; it's simply a part of their creative DNA, the way they are.

To be a great choreographer (or teacher), you have to invest everything you have in your dancers. You have to be so devoted to them and to the finished creation that your dancers become your heroes. It takes courage to be generous like that, to believe that the better the dancers look (or the actors in your film, or the singers of your song), the better the scene will play and the more satisfying the work itself will be. Without that generosity, you'll always hold something back. The finished work shows it, and your audience knows it.

It took me years to appreciate this. When I was younger (read: more limber, athletic, and strong) I used to do this awful thing to myself: Whatever dance I was working on, I would literally put myself in the center of the piece, even though I knew full well that I wasn't going to get to perform it. For a few years there, when I was in my forties and could still move well, I would get really pissy when the inevitable moment arrived and I would have to recuse myself from the piece and hand it over to one of my dancers. Of course, injecting myself into the piece was one of the ways I identified what the piece was about. (Every director does this—tries each role on herself.) But each advancing year taught me a little more about generosity. Nearing my sixth decade, I could no longer rationally harbor illusions that I was the only one who could perform my work. In fact, I couldn't. If I could, it would not have been challenging enough for my extraordinary (read: younger) dancers. Age forced me to learn how to give everything to my dancers. That's not an easy lesson to learn, but I'm grateful for it. (Still pissed off, but grateful.)

I cannot overstate how much a generous spirit contributes to good luck. Look at the luckiest people around you, the ones you envy, the ones who seem to have destiny falling habitually into their laps. What are they doing that singles them out? It isn't dumb luck if it happens repeatedly. If they're anything like the fortunate people I know, they're prepared, they're always working at their craft, they're alert, they involve their friends in their work, and they tend to make others feel lucky to be around them.

19 Work with the Best

If it's true that who you are now and who you will be in five years depend on what books you read and which people you meet, then you need to think more aggressively about those you invite into your creative life. New collaborators bring new vectors of energy into your static world—and they can be combustible. When people say they have good chemistry with others, they're not using the lab metaphor loosely. Their molecules bounce off your molecules.

It doesn't matter what genre you work in, you need to rub up against other people. If you're a composer, it's your collaborators on lyrics, or the singer, or the members of your band (think Mozart without Da Ponte, Verdi without Boito, Rodgers without Hammerstein, Lennon without McCartney). If you're a playwright, it's an actor for whom you want to write a great role or a director who knows how to put your work on the stage. If you're a novelist, it's an editor with helpful suggestions or a friendly reader who can locate your voice. If you're a painter, it's a model who inspires you. It can be a gallery owner who eagerly shows your work, a producer who wants to record your songs, a foundation adviser who gives you a grant, a club owner who lets your band take the stage, a theater manager who gives you space to rehearse and perform—somewhere along the line, you're going to need the contributions and judgment of other people. It's a worthwhile exercise: Work with the best people you can find.

It's easy to think of Igor Stravinsky, for example, as a dedicated, productive, energetic composer working in a vacuum. The truth is quite the opposite. Stravinsky had impeccable taste (and luck) in the people he invited into his creative orbit. In his early years he was tapped by the century's greatest impresario, Sergey Diaghilev, to compose for the Ballets Russes. This gave the young composer a reason to produce such masterpieces as *Petrouchka* and *Firebird* and his revolutionary *Le sacre du printemps.* It also provided him with a venue to have his music heard by people who could appreciate it. Through Diaghilev, he later teamed up with Pablo Picasso to create the ballet *Pulcinella.* He created the opera *Oedipus Rex* with the French poet Jean Cocteau, *Perséphone* with the novelist André Gide, and *The Rake's Progress* with W. H. Auden. Diaghilev, Picasso, Cocteau, Gide, Auden—an impressive roster, confirming that Stravinsky's talent for finding great partners was equal to his gift for composition. His most fruitful collaboration was with George Balanchine; he composed music for more than a dozen Balanchine ballets over a forty-year period, finding in Balanchine a creative equal who could add dramatic resonance to his most intricate scores. This was also shrewd: As long as Balanchine had a dance company, Stravinsky's music would be performed.

In my career, I've collaborated with artists from David Byrne to Milos Forman to Jerome Robbins to Philip Glass. This didn't happen by accident. But it made good accidents happen.

Chapter 8

spine

I once made the mistake of announcing that a new ballet was based on Euripides' *The Bacchae.* It was a mistake because after the first performance, everyone asked me "Where was *The Bacchae?*" Frankly, by then I was so immersed in what the dancers were doing onstage, I, too, had lost track of Euripides. *The Bacchae* had been compelling source material that I latched on to as the spine of the piece when I started choreographing. But that's all it was— an initial impulse for the core of a ballet, not what the ballet became. I realize now that a Greek tragedy was too much information for the audience to handle; it was okay for me to think it, but an audience would find it a distraction. Instead of enjoying the dance, they sat in their seats looking for its skeletal frame. Yet for me, the spine was an essential preparatory step in the ballet's creation. Without it, there would be no starting point, no coherence, no North Star to guide me—and ultimately no dance. My only mistake was that I should have kept it to myself.

Spine, to put it bluntly, begins with your first strong idea. You were scratching to come up with an idea, you found one, and through the next stages of creative thinking you nurtured it into the spine of your creation. The idea is the toehold that gets you started. The spine is the statement you make to yourself outlining your intentions for the work. You intend to tell this story. You intend to explore this theme. You intend to employ this structure. The audience may infer it or not. But if you stick to your spine, the piece will work.

As I mentioned earlier, my Bacchae-inspired dance, *Surfer at the River Styx*, began when Jerome Robbins suggested I choreograph a piece to the Euripides play. I don't usually accept unsolicited advice from other choreographers, but Jerry was a close friend and collaborator, and I knew him to be singularly shrewd about narrative-driven ideas. After all, he was the man who placed Romeo and Juliet on Manhattan's West Side. He definitely knew a good story when he saw it. In effect, he did my scratching for me.

So I reread *The Bacchae*, a story (in twelve words or less) about a king who flouts the god Dionysus and pays for it dearly. The story line was rich with conflict and tension (valuable elements in any staged piece), but I didn't have the forces to flesh out the play's characters and its large, essential chorus. I needed to scale it down to accommodate my small troupe of six dancers. I asked myself, What is the essence of *The Bacchae*? My answer was hubris— that most compelling of tragic flaws. The king, Pentheus, rejects the divinity of Dionysus, who takes vengeance by driving mad his followers, the Bacchae (women worshippers of Bacchus, another name for Dionysus), who then tear Pentheus to pieces. Pentheus's hubris, by itself, is not much of a story (although it does lead to his death), but it was enough of an idea to get me started. As I began casting the piece and creating steps for the dancers, this flimsy tendon of an idea gradually turned into the solid spine of a narrative arc: Dionysus poses as a humble man, and from this stance he regains his status as a deity. Humility conquers hubris, and a god is resurrected. That would be the spine of the piece.

With the principal roles in place (if only in my mind), I thought about how to represent the conflict between the two. For no good reason I had begun to think of my small chorus of four dancers as a river. That's it, I thought: I would place one character (in this case, Dionysus) in consort with the river; the king would

143

be in conflict with the river. The river became the controlling image for the dance, a template for defining the movement of the entire cast.

By the time I had transformed my chorus into a river, I had traveled a long way from *The Bacchae,* and I'm not surprised that my reference to it left that first audience confused. But in my mind the origin and the final outcome are inextricable. You can see *Surfer* a hundred times and never know the role Euripides played in its creation. But I know he's in there, and without him there would be no piece.

I believe that every work of art needs a spine—an underlying theme, a motive for coming into existence. It doesn't have to be apparent to the audience. But you need it at the start of the creative process to guide you and keep you going.

This hit me years ago when I read Bernard Malamud's first novel, *The Natural.* It's the story of an aging baseball player named Roy Hobbes whose promising career was derailed by a woman with a gun. He returns mysteriously to the major leagues after two decades, nearing forty, to play for the ailing New York Knights. He brings his own bat, which he calls Wonderboy, and quickly becomes a hitting sensation. He restores the team, then disappears as mysteriously as he appeared. Strange things happen in the book. Lightning strikes a baseball bat to give it astonishing powers. Losing streaks take on the tragic grandeur of droughts. But more than anything, it's a classic baseball yarn.

Many people know that Malamud drew some of his story from a real incident in the middle of the 1949 season: All-Star first baseman Eddie Waitkus was shot in a hotel room by a woman he had never met before. Though that's as much of the real-life Waitkus as the novelist borrowed, the tale surely served as an inspiration to Malamud. An inspiration, but not his spine.

I would not have realized the distinction in the case of *The Natural* if not for a scholarly friend who told me, "You know it's based on the quest for the Holy Grail, don't you?" In the tones of the English professor he was, he told me about the myth of the Fisher King and drew out all the parallels between Malamud's tale and the myth. The team was named the *Knights,* a nod to Arthurian legend. The team manager was Pop *Fisher.* The hero's first name, *Roy,* is an analogue for "king." And so on. These were not coincidences. Malamud was intentionally making a connection between baseball myth and an equally powerful mythic story from centuries before. Waitkus's story was the idea he had scratched for, the one that got him started; the Grail myth was his spine.

I'm not sure knowing this deepened my appreciation for the book, which was already considerable, but it made Malamud's achievement even more impressive. It also clarified for me the difference between story and theme and spine. Malamud's *story* was a simple baseball yarn. His *theme,* as I discerned it, was redemption. And his *spine* was that search for the Grail.

Somewhere in the triad of story, theme, and spine were permanent distinctions that applied to my work. I rarely have a story to tell—although I recall playwright John Guare saying that every tale tells one of two stories: Romeo and Juliet, or David and Goliath—but I always have a spine.

There's an obvious reason why, as a choreographer, I am constantly groping for a spine. Dance is preverbal; it doesn't have the writer's advantage of using language to establish meaning and intent. The vocabulary of dance is movement, not words. So I need something more in the form of an idea, an image, a memory, a metaphor to make my intentions comprehensible to the audience. I have to articulate this to myself because I won't be using words to articulate it in public.

(Let me hasten to add that I don't think of movement as being poorer than language in conveying meaning. What movement lacks in specificity it more than makes up for in primal power.)

Before I made the spine a habitual part of my creative preparation, I used to agonize through rehearsal periods. If rehearsals weren't going well, I would be dimly aware of it, but I wouldn't know why specifically. I would have a vague feeling of dissatisfaction during the rehearsal ("This isn't working.") and a more clearly etched feeling of emptiness and despair afterward ("I stink. I'll never do anything good again."). It was a horrible feeling, like walking through a thick fog.

I gained one of my earliest introductions to spine when I worked with figure skater John Curry, the 1976 Olympic gold medalist. Curry was a great athlete who wanted his skating to come as close to art as possible within the boundaries of the sport. He showed me that the three components in every athletic performance were the warm-up, the action, and the cooldown. These three components became the spine of the piece I created for him. I put John's daily three-part routine into a dance. It starts out slowly (to allow the athlete to get loose and warm, and to strengthen the muscles and tendons for what they'll have to do next), evolves into a middle section of strenuous, crowd-pleasing leaps and turns requiring maximum exertion, and ends with Curry cooling down in one long continuous glide, elegantly placed on one leg as his momentum slows, then stops as if by magic in the center of the ice.

The warm-up/action/cooldown became the spine of the piece. It worked for me because it reflected a physical truth: This is how athletes function. I have no idea if the audience could see it as clearly as I orchestrated it; if they noticed the structural underpinnings, they were not watching John skate. In the end, whether they see it is not part of the deal I've made with the audience. The spine is my little secret. It keeps me on message, but it is not the message itself.

Everyone who presents his or her work to the public eventually realizes that there is a quasi-legal transaction between artist and audience. A writer, for example, establishes the genre he works in, and you, the reader, agree to its terms. It's a contract between the two of you. A humorist promises to make you laugh. A thriller writer promises to create evil and then conquer it. A mystery writer promises to build a murderous maze and then show you the way out. A romance novelist promises to make you cry. You feel gypped when the author breaks the contract.

It's the same with my audience. We have a contract binding us with an implicit promise. My promise is not merely to entertain the audience with beautiful bodies moving in space—that's the deal all dance audiences take for granted. My promise is to connect them to universal emotions and ancestral impulses through dance. That is why I struggle mightily at the start of any work to connect with roots and first causes and my most ancient memories. I can signal my intentions in many ways, even through the title. If I call a piece *Surfer at the River Styx,* the puzzled audience will at least get the hint that something ancient and mythic is happening onstage.

You might not see your work this way. You might not struggle for spine. You might be content to receive any random thought floating through the ether that happens to settle on you that day. You might think you don't need a supporting mechanism for the art you're constructing, a controlling image, a collateral idea to guide you. You might think getting lost is a big part of the adventure.

You may think that, but you'd be wrong.

Floating spinelessly can get you through the day, but at some point you'll be lost in the middle of a project, whether it's a painting, a novel, a song, or a poem, and you won't know how to get back to what you're trying to accomplish. It might not happen in your first creation, which, in your bubble of sweet inexperience, may skim from heart to mind to canvas, page, or stage exactly as you intended, perfect in shape, proportion, and meaning (in which case, consider yourself blessed). But it will happen in the next piece, or the one after that. It happens to everyone. You'll find yourself pacing your particular white room, asking yourself, What am I trying to say? That is the moment when you will embrace, with gratitude, the notion of a spine.

Keep in mind that coming up with a spine is neither a chore nor a distraction that takes you away from the real work of the creative process. It is a tool, a gift you give yourself to make your job easier. As for the particular quality of your spine, I'm not concerned with how you've developed it or how you exploit it; your choice of spine is as personal as how you pray. It's a private choice that only has to provide comfort and guidance to you. It's your spine. Use what works for you.

You can discover the spine of a piece in many ways.

You can find it with the aid of a **friend.** That's what editors do for writers who have lost their way. It's the editor's job to challenge writers who are handing in stories with shaky narratives and lazy sentences. The question is always

"What are you trying to say?" (In such cases, the editor is functioning as a chiropractor, bringing the spine back into proper alignment.)

You can induce it with a ritual. I know a lawyer who has a useful gambit when questioning his clients: Whenever he hears a muddled explanation, he holds up his hands to silence the speaker and says, "Okay, explain it to me as if I'm ten years old." That simple instruction, perhaps because it floods people with memories of a simpler time, gets them talking with clarity and purpose. That's what the spine is to me: It's my explanation to myself as if I'm ten years old again.

You can also discover the spine by recalling your original intentions and clarifying your goals. What was the first thing you dropped into your box for the project? Go back to it and remember how you started—that's what it's there for.

"Make them laugh" was the original impulse for an early piece of mine, *Eight Jelly Rolls,* set to the witty tunes of Jelly Roll Morton. Whenever I wavered in my intentions, I could always return to the home thought: Is it funny? Will they laugh?

For a later piece, *Baker's Dozen,* my spine was a portrait of communities and how they function together positively. The key word is *positively.* In my mind I kept the image of Edward Hicks's *The Peaceable Kingdom*—his famous painting of the beasts of the world together in blissful coexistence, lion beside ox, wolf next to lamb. That was the level of harmony I was aiming for. Whenever the piece, set to Willie "the Lion" Smith recordings, threatened to take a dark turn, I snapped it back to my sunny intentions: twelve dancers representing an ideal society, not a tortured one. It must have worked. The audience always leaves grinning.

For a later dance, *Nine Sinatra Songs,* the spinal thought was the life of a married couple from beginning (infatuation and passion) to end (ongoing acceptance). The story was silent, told by seven dancing couples, but the audience certainly picked up on it, cued in part by the lyrics of the songs. It became one of my biggest successes.

Sometimes the spine does **double duty,** both as the covert idea guiding the artist and the overt theme for the audience. That's what makes Herman Melville's *Moby-Dick* so powerful and enduring. It has a solid unrelenting spine: get the whale. And that spine totally supports the novel's theme: obsession—get the whale. It is so clear and strong that readers stick with the book through all of Melville's detours into ivory carving and sail making and Atlantic weather patterns. They know the author's intentions. And they want to know if Ahab gets the whale.

Sometimes the spine of a piece comes from the music I've chosen. For example, I love to create dances in the form of theme and variations. In many ways, this genre is a perfect blueprint for organizing a dance: Each new variation is my cue to change dancers or groupings or steps. It makes my job a lot easier if the music tells me where to end one section and begin another. (Can you blame me for picking a form that gives me one less variable to worry about?) As a result, I have gladly tackled the behemoths of the form: Brahms's *Handel Variations,* and his *Haydn Variations* and *Paganini Variations,* too, and the most intimidating set of all, Beethoven's *Diabelli Variations.*

Musicologists have written books devoted solely to analyzing the mathematical complexities of this masterpiece from Beethoven's later years. In 1819 the music publisher Anton Diabelli sent a simple waltz theme to every composer he could think of, inviting each to contribute one variation. The resulting work would be an anthology of contemporary music in all its guises.

Beethoven, that classic overachiever, initially tried his hand at eight to twelve of them, after first saying he wasn't going to do any. (Remember, he was only asked to contribute *one.*) Diabelli's theme, he concluded, was so laughably simple and amateurish, he wanted nothing to do with it. But the theme must have lodged in his head and taken root, because three years later, while he was composing his last piano sonata, Op. 111, he realized he was using the Diabelli theme, and that discovery sent him back to the project. He wound up writing a series of variations now formally known as *Thirty-Three Variations on a Waltz by*

Diabelli, C Major, Op. 120. This gigantic composition for solo piano, nearly one hour in length, does not stray from the original theme. A sophisticated listener who can read music and understand composition is never lost because Diabelli's theme is the spine of the piece and the spine stays intact in each variation. Beethoven has so much invention that he can transform the theme without losing it. In the first variation, he alters the original time signature from a 3/4 waltz to a 4/4 march. He also slows it down; it's the same number of bars but twice as long. He hooks you by repeating the same structure and then shakes you up by transforming it in ways that leave you gasping. That's the magic. He created huge extremes, going from sforzando to pianissimo, developing dramatic effects that helped define the Romantic style. He creates a tension that's almost tactile. As the variations unfold, you wonder with awe and amazement, "What's next? Can he do another?"

My challenge was to match Beethoven's notes with my steps. Can I do it? Can I keep up?

The key for me was to make my theme simple and serviceable. To set this music to dance, I needed a spine that would make sense of Beethoven's daunting architecture and keep me grounded. Variations, by definition, begin with a theme and alter it. The wealth of techniques for varying the theme without destroying it creates the beauty of the form. I, too, could create a theme, expand it, turn it upside down, turn it inside out, or flip it front to back. I, too, could do all kinds of imaginable operations to it, translating all that music into movement. But eventually I would have to return home, like a prodigal son. That, I decided, would be my spine: Bring it home. I thought of Beethoven's variations as a journey in which the hero (the original theme) leaves home, grows, matures, and then returns. If I could suggest that in dance, I would have the perfect analogue to the sweeping arc of Beethoven's composition.

I also learned from Beethoven's deep well of invention how useful a simple melody could be. Just as Diabelli's tune became Beethoven's spine, I developed a choreographic equivalent of that tune (a series of skips, hops, and stops) that would serve me as well and would recur throughout the piece. I wasn't mimicking Beethoven; I was running parallel to his music.

Another part of the spine would be to figure out how the original has been changed and how it has profited from the journey. If its innocence is still intact, the piece is a comedy. If its innocence is lost and it hasn't profited from the experience, the piece is a tragedy. When the source material that provides your spine is as clear as tragedy or comedy to you, then your foundation is sound and will mean something to others.

Once you accept the power of spine in the creative act, you will become much more efficient in your creativity. You will still get lost on occasion, but having a spine will anchor you. When you lose your way, it will show you the way home. It will remind you that this is what you have set out to do, this is the story you're trying to tell, this is the effect you're trying to achieve. Having a spine will snap you back to attention quickly and, as a result, will inject speed and economy into your work habits. Energy and time are finite resources; conserving them is very important.

I've always thought that one of the great rewards of being a creative person is that *I get to do it*. Like a writer who enjoys the process of knocking out the words at his or her desk (on good days), or the artist who can spend all day in the studio because he loves the mechanical act of applying paint onto canvas (on good days), I love being in a dance studio creating steps with dancers (on good days). I know writers who say they take little pleasure in *writing* but they love *having written*. I'm not like that. I'm more like the athlete who enjoys practicing as much as playing the actual game. I get a kick out of the sweat and rigor and sheer exertion of making my body move, whether it's in the studio or in performance. If you have trouble appreciating this, imagine people dancing into the wee hours of the morning at a club. Most of them have spent all day working at demanding jobs. Yet their energy returns like magic at night when the music and dancing start up. Dancing, perhaps more than any other art form, has an energizing effect on people.

But there's a danger here. The sheer pleasure of working in the studio introduces the temptation to linger, to fall in love with the process of creation rather than driving toward the end product. Take this sort of thing to an extreme and you'll never finish anything.

This is where having a solid spine is invaluable. Having a spine lets me know where I am starting from and where I want to go. It's easy to forget this when you're enjoying yourself so much in the middle. In this sense, I think of spine as an efficiency expert holding a stopwatch as I work. It lets me know when I am dawdling or digressing or wasting time. It reminds me that everything I add is either on message or off. Most of all, it lets me know when I'm done.

I take my cues in this regard from Buster Keaton. What I like about Keaton is how simply he got to where he wanted to go. His productivity was extraordinary, in large part because he always had a clear idea of where to start and where to finish. He had an economy of purpose and execution, which I attribute to having a strong spine in his work. You could argue that all of his comic set pieces had the same spine: Get the last laugh. He knew that the payoff, the one big laugh, always came at the end, when he fell down a hole or slipped on a banana peel or watched everything come crashing down around him. Keaton knew that you don't get the laugh when you set the scene up. You don't get the laugh while you're developing it during the middle section. You get the laugh at the end, when you actually hit the deck. It wasn't that Keaton rushed a scene, but he was very economical about the middle. (Some scenes took their time. In the leisurely opening of the 1921 short film *The Goat,* a starving Keaton is sent to the back of a breadline; he doesn't realize he's standing behind two mannequins, so for perhaps the first time in film history we watch a character wait.)

In another short I think of Keaton standing on the street. On the balcony above is a girl he longs for. He scribbles a love note to her, folds it into an airplane, and sends it up to her. The camera stays on Keaton for a few moments, and then the paper comes floating back to him torn into little snowflakes. He turns his collar up to protect himself from the cold. That's pure Keaton: He gets from the premise of the scene (would-be lover is rebuffed) to the punch line (the chill from paper snowflakes) with extraordinary economy of mood and action.

That technique was his spine.

Years ago I spent a lot of time studying Keaton's films, trying to understand how he achieved his effects and hoping to do the same in my work. Patterns emerged. There was always a disaster in Keaton's films, and he always survived. And there was always a moment in which he endured and suffered and waited for disaster to strike. I saw method in his mayhem. The story line may change from film to film, but Keaton had a theme (disaster strikes) and he had a spine (survive—to get the last laugh). He didn't waste much time in the middle. He went from cause to effect as quickly as possible. The directness of his method can be summed up in his most famous stunt, the falling wall sequence from *Steamboat Bill, Jr.* He's standing in front of a wall that's about to come crashing down; he doesn't know it, but we do. We see it falling down onto him—but someone's left a window open, and so the wall falls to the ground *around him.*

153

What gives the punch line such impact is that it's a surprise. We ask ourselves, "Why didn't I see that?" We didn't see it because Keaton didn't give us time to think about it. He was getting on with it, not waiting. That's my ideal version of spine. Whenever I find myself wandering down blind alleys, veering away from my spine, I think of Keaton and his straight path to the end.

Keep these images in mind whenever you work on developing the spine of a piece, if only to remind you that the process of creating can be thrilling and exciting—and will work better if you can get to the good parts as quickly as possible.

I could go on about spines, but that's also the point: Every piece I make now has a spine. It's habitual. It's helpful. And it keeps me on my toes.

exercises

20 Make a Picture That's Worth Ten Thousand Words

If a picture is worth a thousand words, then dance, because it moves, may be worth ten thousand.

I take comfort in Ludwig Wittgenstein's observation of the resemblance among the various forms that music takes on. "The gramophone record, the musical thought, the score, the waves of sound, all stand to one another in that pictorial internal relation, which holds between language and the world. To all of them the logical structure is common." Wittgenstein was pointing out that there are affinities between seemingly different objects that we comprehend pictorially but cannot verbalize. It is, after all, hard to express how musical thought and sound waves and the undulating scratchings of eighth notes and quarter notes on a sheet of music resemble one another. Each relies on different material and a different grammar. Yet we sense they are saying the same thing. We sense that they share a common structure, because we see and hear the waves.

Dance has that power of making us see and feel affinities.

Take the White Swan's last exit in Act II of *Swan Lake*. The ballerina turns her back to the audience, facing Albrecht, her prince, and bourrées across the stage with her arms extended at her sides. As she executes her delicate journey on the points of her toes across the stage, a ripple of movement begins at her left hand's fingertips and continues through all the joints of her left arm, her shoulders and back, through all the

155

joints of her right arm to her right hand's fingertips. The ripple then returns from right to left, again and again, until the undulating gesture accumulates power and creates a burning image of a wave. It is one of the most marvelous moments of beauty and heartbreak in the entire ballet canon. It never fails to elicit a gasp from the audience. It is a gasp of wonder and sorrow. We immediately sense that this ripple is a metaphor for the fluttering of bird's wings. The ballerina is, after all, portraying a swan. But the exquisite move across the stage also reminds us of the wavelike motion of the water supporting this ballerina-swan. And her gesture suggests so much more. Is the swan waving good-bye to her prince? Or is she beckoning him? "Come with me." Or is the ripple a gesture of resignation, her final spasm of life? Or is it all of the above?

Someone in the audience could write ten thousand words about this single moment in a three-hour ballet. That's how rich movement can be.

Now it's your turn. Do your version of the White Swan scene. Create a gesture or movement that would need many words to convey its meaning. It could be something like the Italian gesture of putting thumb to fingertips, palm upraised, and bouncing your hand. If you had to explain this in writing, what would it mean? (Early in *Movin' Out,* a character mimes kicking a field goal and raising his hands above his head to signal "Score!" The move takes 1.3 seconds, but it suggests everything—football, Saturday afternoons, high school, girls and boys, cars, youth.)

If you can do this, you have the skill to develop congruities and affinities. If you have that skill, you can always find spine. When words fail, spine does not.

21 Spinal Tap

Pick a favorite work of art and try to determine what spine, if any, the artist built into it. It could be a novel, movie, painting, play, opera, ballet, cartoon, TV sitcom, whatever. This is an exercise in seeking out the hidden architecture of a piece.

Some artists give you strong hints, such as the quest myth spine of Malamud's *The Natural,* that only become obvious when studied or revealed outright.

Others make it easy for you. The German novelist Thomas Mann offers a field day for would-be spinal tappers. His first novel, *Buddenbrooks,* is clearly built around the spine of a decaying organism; we watch a family dynasty as it disappears. A later novel, the sprawling *Joseph and His Brothers,* takes its plot literally and directly from the Old Testament's Book of Exodus. Mann's novel itself is fourteen hundred pages long, but the spine of the book is a Bible story covering just a few pages, Joseph's enslavement in Egypt. In *Doctor Faustus,* Mann makes no effort to hide the fact that the Faust legend provides the infrastructure for his story about a composer who sells his soul to the devil in exchange for fourteen years of unbridled creativity. The spine is right there in the title.

I happen to like these books, so I'm attuned to the authors' motives and methods. You can do the same with works that speak to you. Just because they are literary doesn't make their spines any easier to gauge than that of a symphony or painting. If the work matters to you, you will eventually discern the material the artist built upon.

Entering into the convolutions of an artist's mind can be as bewildering as trying to explain a dream. But this is an exercise, not a test; there are no right or wrong answers here. The spine is one of the first places to look if you want to understand how a work of art gathers substance and integrity. If you can find the spine in work that already speaks to you, you can build better spines for work of your own.

22 What's Your MQ?

The process by which we transform the meaning of one thing into something different is an essential part of human intelligence. Without symbols, and the ability to understand them, there would be no writing, no numbers, no drama, no art. Everything you create is a representation of something else; in this sense, everything you create is enriched by metaphor.

Developing a spine is the first step in building what I like to think of as your MQ, or metaphor quotient. In the creative process, MQ is as valuable as IQ.

You get an inkling of this in tests constructed to measure intelligence. Many of these challenge your capacity to recognize and construct metaphor. Take a question like "*Canyon* is to *bridge* as *mountain* is to (a) *cave*, (b) *mine*, (c) *peak*, (d) *ridge*, or (e) *tunnel*." The question is designed to test your ability to see patterns where patterns don't obviously exist and then to re-create them. A bridge lets people get to the other side of a canyon in the same way that a tunnel lets people get to the other side of a mountain. Much about IQ tests revolves around comparing—comparing a series of five objects to determine *which does not belong* or comparing a sequence of three drawings and choosing a fourth that *completes the sequence*. Comparing is the engine that drives metaphor.

Let's take it a step further with these seven exercises. They won't tell you how smart you are, but if they bring you more in touch with all the metaphor around you, they can change the way you think.

1. How many images and objects can you see in three minutes of cloud gazing? This is metaphor as visual translation.

2. While doing a "mindless" chore, like washing the dishes, try to become the rhythm of the process. What's the rhythm of scrub, wash, or rinse? Hum the rhythm. Give it a name. What other "mindless" chores have a matching rhythm? This is metaphor as object or task.

3. Distill a mechanical sound and mimic it. For example, take the click-click of a blinking turn signal in a car. Lock the tempo and beat within you and then mimic it when you speak. Now hear the beat in other people speaking. Then see how the world begins to move to your beat. (This happened to me one day in a taxi on my way to rehearsal. The turn signal clicking worked its way inside my head. It made me think of kids skipping rope, which led to an image of kids skipping double Dutch. That positioning made me think of dancers standing on opposite sides of a line onstage; I used the image that day at rehearsal, while it was still in my head. All from a turn signal.) This is metaphor as aural and visual stimulus.

4. "Step on a crack, break your mother's back." Do you ever find yourself behaving superstitiously in order to control your destiny? Focus on a superstition, like knocking on wood to bring yourself luck or tossing salt over your shoulder to fend off evil spirits. What image springs to mind? A happy ending or the devil? Follow your thoughts wherever they lead. This is metaphor as faith.

5. Study a word's linguistic roots. Where does it take you? How far back must you go? What are you thinking about when you come to the source? For example, the word *tragedy* always makes me think of goats. Tragedy derives from the Greek *trages,* which means goat. In ancient times, goats were used as sacrifices to the gods. The story goes that some goats ate the grape leaves in a vineyard of the gods, thus offending the deities. The goats took the fall. Eventually the Greeks stopped sacrificing valuable goats and, in their place, created rituals and plays to appease the gods. Heroes replaced goats, but the actors were only killed symbolically. Their characters took the fall. The plays were known as tragedies, after the goats. This is metaphor as theater.

6. Find two works of art you can connect to each other. What is the connection? Is this what the creators intended, or are you seeing something they didn't or perhaps couldn't see? You are making the works your own by putting them together in new and interesting ways. For example, I saw a blockbuster Picasso/Matisse exhibition that succeeded in demonstrating incredible parallels between the two painters. But what interested me more than the comparisons was my realization that Matisse would never have created his late-period paper cutouts if not for Picasso's youthful paper collages done thirty years earlier. I had always thought that cutouts were Matisse's invention. This exhibition suggested otherwise. The connection was a revelation to me. This is metaphor as curating.

7. Turn Narcissus around. Try to see another person in your image. Then reverse it and try to see yourself in that person's image. Imagine your life if you had that person's wealth (or looks, or taste, or biases) or that person had yours. This is metaphor as empathy. And it's a common one. You're walking the proverbial mile in someone else's shoes. People do this every day (in its uglier incarnation, it is known as envy).

Metaphor is all around you. It's never too late to raise your MQ.

Chapter 9

skill

Pope Leo X heard that Leonardo da Vinci was experimenting with the formulas for varnishes instead of executing a painting. He declared, "This man will never do anything, for he begins thinking about the end before the beginning of his work."

However, Leonardo understood that the better you know the nuts and bolts of your craft, the more fully you can express your talents.

The great painters are incomparable draftsmen. They also know how to mix their own paint, grind it, put in the fixative; no task is too small to be worthy of their attention.

The great composers are usually dazzling musicians. They have to know their instrument before they can make it sing the tune in their head. Johann Sebastian Bach took this further, learning how to build organs as a young man and becoming one of Europe's leading experts on its sound. He literally knew the instrument inside and out.

A great chef can chop and dice better than anyone in his kitchen.

The best fashion designers are invariably virtuosos with a needle and thread. Even when they have armies of assistants preparing their designs, they still know how to cut and sew better than anyone working for them.

The best writers are well-read people. They have the richest appreciation of words, the biggest vocabularies, the keenest ear for language. They also know their grammar. Words and language are their tools, and they have learned how to use them. (Joseph Epstein blanches with anger and embarrassment when he runs across a word he doesn't know. To him, not knowing a word is like a doctor not knowing the name of an obscure but vital nerve, or a carpenter forgetting the name of a type of nail. Perhaps he's being a bit extreme, too harsh on himself; it's impossible to know all the million-plus words in the English language, but you can't help admiring his desire to know them all.)

A successful entrepreneur can do everything and anything—stock the warehouse, negotiate with vendors, develop a product, design an ad campaign, close a deal, placate an unhappy customer—as well as, if not better than, anyone working for him.

What all these people have in common is that they have mastered the underlying skills of their creative domain, and built their creativity on the solid foundation of those skills.

Skill gives you the wherewithal to execute whatever occurs to you. Without it, you are just a font of unfulfilled ideas. Skill is how you close the gap between what you can see in your mind's eye and what you can produce; the more skill you have, the more sophisticated and accomplished your ideas can be. With absolute skill comes absolute confidence, allowing you to dare to be simple. Picasso once said, while admiring an exhibition of children's art, "When I was their age I could draw like Raphael, but it has taken me a whole lifetime to learn to draw like them."

You're only kidding yourself if you put creativity before craft. Craft is where our best efforts begin. You should never worry that rote exercises aimed at developing skills will suffocate creativity. At the same time, it's important to recognize that demonstrating great technique is not the same as being creative. Bach, Mozart, and Beethoven were all keyboard virtuosi, but each demanded more of his music than the exploitation of keyboard skill. Beethoven, for example, wrote greater (and more difficult) music in his later years (when his keyboard skills declined) than he did in his youth. The craft in his fingers had diminished but the skill in his head had grown.

An awareness of your particular set of skills will tell you what sets you apart. When asked to explain his success, Billy Joel says, "I have a job where I get to do the only things I'm good at doing. I can sing in tune. I can play an instrument. I can write songs. And I can get on stage and perform. I'm not a virtuoso at any single one. I'm competent and I do my job. But I'm in a field, the music industry, that sees this as extraordinary."

Sometimes the most important skills are forced upon you by other people. The first time I worked with Jennifer Tipton, the lighting designer, was on my very first ballet in 1965, *Tank Dive*. There was a moment in the piece when I told her, "Jenny, at this point you will turn off the lights so I can exit."

"No, I won't," she said. "Get yourself offstage."

I loved her attitude. From then on, I never counted on lighting to do my job for me. It forced me to confront and learn one of the most difficult skills in stage directing: how to get performers on and off the stage. (This is not just an issue for directors and choreographers. The novelist John Gregory Dunne, explaining the difficulties of writing novels, says, "Because one has written other books does not mean the next becomes any easier. Each book in fact is a tabula rasa; from book to book I seem to forget how to get characters in and out of rooms—a far more difficult task than the nonwriter might think.")

Yogi Berra once said that for Christmas he told his father, "I want a baseball bat, a glove, and a ball." His father said, "Which one of the three do you want?" As a good parent, he was saying, I can't give you everything, but if you're really serious about baseball, you'll figure out how to get the other two. That's a powerful lesson: *Learn to do for yourself.* It's the only way to broaden your skills.

Odd as it may sound, personality is a skill. You can choose and develop aspects of it that will draw people to you and make them want to help you learn and improve. When I was playing hooky from college and running every day to a Manhattan dance studio near Carnegie Hall to take classes, Margot Fonteyn came into the dressing room one day wearing a mink coat, with all the accoutrements of the grande dame that she was. This was unheard of in the dancing world as far as I knew. No one was that rich! She looked like an opera star. But then she took out this simple wardrobe—a pair of pink tights and a black leotard—and that was all she wore. She went into the studio and worked in the back. The instructor would always make a point of inviting her to the front, and we would all back off as if to say "This is your room." But she would never move forward. One of her skills, and a great deal of her charm, was this built-in sense of humility. The greatest dancers have that, I learned.

One dancer I know insists her greatest skill is a talent for seduction. She told me that she grew up with a Siamese cat and a Great Dane, and she spent hours watching the cat gain control over the vastly larger dog. It was a life lesson in seduction, and she brings that skill with her every time she takes the stage.

At auditions I find I can size up a dancer and determine if he's right for my company or project by the way he comes in the door and puts his bag down. That and asking him to come forward and move into fifth position will tell me all I need to know about his training, his attitude, his propriety and modesty, even his charisma. If he has the skill, there's no hiding it. Without skill, there is no confidence. You cannot fake it.

Confidence is a trait that has to be earned honestly and refreshed constantly; you have to work as hard to protect your skills as you did to develop them. This means vigilant practice and excellent practice habits. You've heard the phrase "Practice makes perfect"? Not true. *Perfect practice* makes perfect. The one thing that creative souls around the world have in common is that they all have to practice to maintain their skills. Art is a vast democracy of habit.

All dancers lead the same life; the lowliest corps member and the megastar still have to go to the same class at 10:00 A.M. to stay in shape. Painters still have to prepare their own paints. Soloists spend hours at their instruments before they rehearse with the orchestra. These habits don't disappear when you become recognized, honored, rich, famous, and otherwise validated. In fact, though everyone is free to practice as much as they want, it's the most acclaimed and skilled people who work the hardest to maintain those skills. The greatest musical virtuosos spend more hours a day practicing than do the members of an orchestra. Mikhail Baryshnikov was always the hardest-working student at the Kirov school; his teacher Pushkin singled him out for his abilities and made him continue working after everyone went home for the day. He maintained that ethic of working harder than anyone else twenty years later when he was the most admired dancer in the world. It's the same in sports. The greatest (and highest-paid) athletes, like Tiger Woods and Michael Jordan, practice harder, longer, and better than their rivals. Moreover, they extend that discipline to the most basic elements of their craft. Prima ballerinas work as diligently and carefully at the barre as any novice. (Actually they work *more* diligently on basics that lesser dancers might consider beneath them.) The great ones never take fundamentals for granted.

You may wonder which came first: the skill or the hard work. But that's a moot point. The Zen master cleans his own studio. So should you.

The real issue is conditioning. It's an obvious concern for a dancer, who won't return to the studio after two weeks away with the same physical coordination and stamina as when he left. It's not as obvious for a concert pianist, yet I don't know any virtuoso who would take the stage without weeks of preparation and practice. It's the only way to be sharp, even if the performer is the only one in the hall who hears the difference. And a surgeon once told me that he notices if one of his scrub nurses has been off for a week; he can see a fraction of a second difference in the way she reacts to his requests at the operating table. He detects the same lack of acute skill in himself if he has been on vacation for a week or two. It might not be obvious to his colleagues, but he knows it. It takes him a day or two to lose the rustiness.

Practice without purpose, however, is nothing more than exercise. Too many people practice what they're already good at and neglect the skills that need more work. It's pleasant to repeat the things we do well, while it's frustrating to deal with repeated failure. I see this all the time with dancers. If they have great leg extension but deficient arms, they will spend more time working on leg extension (because the effort is rewarding—it looks good and feels good) and less time on their arms. Common sense should tell them the process ought to be reversed. That's what the great ones do: They shelve the perfected skills for a while and concentrate on their imperfections.

The golfer Davis Love III was taught by his father to think of practice as a huge circle, like a clock. You work on a skill until you master it, and then you move on to the next one. When you've mastered that, you move on to the next, and the next, and the next, and eventually you'll come full circle to the task that you began with, which will now need remedial work because of all the time you've spent on other things.

If you do this, you approach a state of mastery, which is the acquisition of consummate skill and technique. But "technique is not enough," writes Jacques Barzun. "Something more is needed—and perhaps something less. Take the music of Saint-Saëns. Here was a precocious, enormously gifted musician; he could turn out pieces that seemed as if written by Mozart or Beethoven or anybody he wished. But as Berlioz, who was his mentor, regretfully remarked, the young man lacked *in*experience."

Every artist faces this paradox. Experience—the faith in your ability and the memory that you have done this before—is what gets you through the door. But experience also closes the door. You tend to rely on that memory and stick with what has worked before. You don't try anything new.

Inexperience is innocence, naïveté, and humility. It is a powerful ignorance that is summed up for me in an obituary I read of the All-American football player Ellis Jones. Jones, who died at age eighty in 2002, lost his right arm in an accident when he was eleven years old. But that didn't stop him from playing guard on offense and linebacker on defense in the 1940s at the University of Tulsa and later in the fledgling National Football League. "I played football before I got hurt," said Jones of the accident that cost him his right arm. "It never occurred to me that I couldn't keep playing. I guess I was too dumb to think I could not do it." Inexperience provides us with a childlike fearlessness that is the polar opposite of the alleged wisdom that age confers on us, the "wisdom" telling us some goals are foolish, a waste of time, invitations to disaster. In its purest form, inexperience erases fear. You do not know what is and is not possible and therefore everything is possible.

It is that perfect moment of equipoise between knowing it all and knowing nothing that Hemingway was straining for when he said, "The thing is to become a master and in your old age to acquire the courage to do what children did when they knew nothing." You cannot manufacture inexperience, but you can maintain it and protect what you have.

Beethoven was constantly switching from one skill set to another. For example, he wrote thirty-two piano sonatas in his lifetime, but he did not write them all in one bunch. He composed piano sonatas at every stage in his career, early, middle, and late. Years would pass when he didn't write any piano sonatas; during those gaps, he turned to symphonies and string quartets and piano trios and concertos. He knew there was a difference between what you could accomplish on a solo piano and the music you could achieve with a full orchestra, and he reveled in the difference and used both. Switching genres was his way of maintaining his inexperience and, as a result, enlarging his art. Whenever he came back to the piano, he would bring to the keyboard everything he had learned from the trios, quartets, concertos, and symphonies. That is why his thirty-second sonata, Op. 111, composed five years before his death, breaks your heart: Everything Beethoven had learned about musical form, ensemble, and masses of sound can be heard in this last sonata.

Consciously or not, I have always followed one dance piece, successful or otherwise, by launching the next as far in the other direction as possible. I will deliberately follow a ballet for a large cast of dancers set to orchestral music with a piece for a small group to pop music or a jazz solo. I'm not interested in repeating my experience. I want to maintain some *inexperience*. Giving my next dance a new set of specs is one sure way to do that. Moving from modern dance to ballet is another. Switching gears from concert halls to Broadway is yet another. Norman Mailer calls this "rotating your crops." Each new challenge is a way to protect your inexperience, make you remember something you never had a chance to forget. When it's all done, you bring it back to your craft, stronger and wiser.

Analyze your own skill set. See where you're strong and where you need dramatic improvement, and tackle those lagging skills first. It's harder than it sounds (most useful habits are), but it's the only way to improve. In *A Book of Five Rings*, the sixteenth-century Japanese swordfighter Miyamoto Musashi counseled, "Never have a favorite weapon." Warriors know they need to enlarge their arsenal of skills in order to avoid becoming predictable to their adversaries. It's no different when the craft is a creative one, and the stakes are somewhat less than life and death. A photographer who can work with both small- and large-format cameras, in a controlled studio and outside in the real world, has exponentially enlarged his potential for developing his career. Likewise, a fiction writer who has mastered the short story and the novel form has more options available in telling a story than a short-story writer who has never flexed his muscles in a novel's long form.

When I'm considering my own skills, I break them down into categories:

Musical skill:

an understanding of musical structure and history.

Dramatic skill:

a sense of what will make people care, with a dollop of daring and flair that surprises people and qualifies as showmanship.

Painterly skill:

the ability to conceive images in two dimensions, which is very much like creating the balances and proportions in a painting.

Sculptural skill:

adding depth and a sense of mass to the painterly skill.

Psychological skill:

knowing the strategies and techniques to get people to do what you want done.

Design skill:

having enough knowledge and taste to communicate collaboratively with set, lighting, and costume designers.

Theatrical skill:

knowing how to sustain the peaks and valleys once you get moving in the right direction.

Temporal skill:

feeling time in your gut, so you know when a scene or phrase has
gone on long enough.

Motivational skill:

making people want to work with you and for you.

Entrepreneurial skill:

getting the project up in front of people.

Promotional skill:

keeping it going after the first performance.

Athletic skill:

knowing as much as possible about how the body works and moves.

Literary skill:

having a sense of beginning, middle, and end.

A writer might not need sculptural skill, since he doesn't work in three dimensions; most creative endeavors don't require athletic or musical or design skills. Still, I suspect everyone could use at least two-thirds of these categories to get the most out of his or her efforts.

(Of course, there's an *ur*-skill that I don't even feel obliged to list. That, dear reader, is *discipline*. Everyone needs it. No explanation required.)

The skills you've developed suffuse all aspects of your ability to create. The white-hot pitch of creativity is only useful to the person who knows what to do with it. In his notebooks, in discussing the power of the crossbow, Leonardo da Vinci makes reference to doubling its degrees of "fury" through applied technique and dexterity. This is a useful metaphor for your creative efforts: *You double your intensity with skill.*

Before taking on a subject, Leonardo would consider it from an extraordinary number of directions. He had a poetic feel for scientific imagery. Take his description of waves upon the water:

Observe the motion of the surface of the water, how it resembles that of hair, which has two movements—one depends on the weight of the hair, the other on the direction of the curls; thus the water forms whirling eddies, one part following the impetus of the chief current, and the other following the incidental motions and return flow.

Leonardo's breadth of interests was remarkable. So was his ability to bounce back from one area of study to another and find relationships between them. This refreshed him, kept alive his passion for the new. Painters, writers, musicians, we all need this breadth and passion if we're going to keep perfecting our craft, whether or not there is approval, validation, or money coming from it.

I saw this when I worked with Baryshnikov. He was the most skilled classical dancer of his time; there was nothing he couldn't do in the classical repertoire. Yet overriding all this ability was an enormous romantic desire to perform American dance. It's the reason he left his country and family and defected to America. In hindsight, his success in the West looks like a no-brainer, but it wasn't that obvious back in 1975 when he and I first met and worked together on the jazzy *Push Comes to Shove*. I could have easily given him a flashy dance with leaps and turns that took advantage of his great technique. It would have thrilled the audience—but it would have disappointed him. His desire to dance something new and different was overwhelming. He had turned his life upside down to fulfill that passion. So, while I did invent jumps and pirouettes for him (you have to let your thoroughbreds run at some point), I also gave him a character to play—the master of ceremonies, complete with hat—that he regarded as very American, practically vaudevillian. He took the character and somehow this great dancer made himself appear as an underdog to the audience—very vulnerable, very appealing. All because of his extreme passion to dance in a way he considered American.

Without passion, all the skill in the world won't lift you above craft. Without skill, all the passion in the world will leave you eager but floundering. Combining the two is the essence of the creative life.

exercises

23 Take Inventory of Your Skills

Before you can appreciate your skills and where you might need improvement, you need to take inventory. This is tougher than it sounds. Where do you begin? With basic skills you take for granted (like walking and talking), or the specific skills that enhance your craft? To help you get started, I asked my dance troupe to describe a successful dancer's skill set. Here's what they came up with:

Obviously there is the *athletic component.* Dancers have to be exceptional athletes. And under *athletic* would be the basic skills of coordination, balance, poise, flexibility, endurance, and strength. These are so basic that dancers forget to mention them; moving and its component parts are like breathing to them.

Then there's *acting skill.* Dancers have to display a sense of timing and the ability to play a character.

Musicality is also a skill. Dancers have to move in rhythm with the music and also know how to phrase against it.

Perseverance is a big skill, too. The dancer's life is tougher than most. It's just like acting or singing, only in addition to remembering your lines and performing, you have to train like a prizefighter for four or more hours a day to maintain your athletic skills.

Discipline goes hand in hand with perseverance.

So does a *sense of humor.* Every great dancer has this, or at least a sense of the absurd. To a visitor from Mars, it's a bizarre and silly art we pursue. We stand on one leg rather than two, we float our arms overhead rather than keep them at our sides, we spin on our toes trying to convince people that these movements are beautiful.

Then there is the refinement of these skills, like *physical intelligence,* by which I mean an awareness of how your body moves in space. There are also good *reflexes,* which are genetic gifts in the form of fast-twitch muscle fibers that can also be enhanced. As a choreographer I particularly value a dancer's ability to *function well in a group.* I look for dancers who can work independently and yet also pull together as a team. *Partnering* is a subset of this but maybe even more valuable for a dancer's career; if you can't partner, you'll rarely find work. So is the *willingness to take direction,* a skill noticed mostly when absent.

Dancers are also *masters of illusion.* In this category the paradigm is Fred Astaire. Ginger Rogers supposedly once asked him why he worked so hard; he replied, "To make it look easy." He worked on *everything.* For example, Astaire had very large hands of which he was extremely self-conscious. He would work for hours in front of mirrors to see exactly what his hands were doing and how they looked. He constructed the illusion of a man who was completely at ease with his body and his movements, as if he were acting totally on impulse, and yet nothing was unscripted, unrehearsed, or out of his control.

Political skill also stands out. The dance world is ruthless. What it takes to survive in a ballet company is very different from what it takes to survive as a gypsy dancer on Broadway. You need shrewd people instincts to handle both worlds and to know their differences.

The final skill I simply list as *forever the child.* You could call it "the ability to not know" or "denial" or "naïveté." It's basically a sense of innocence. You do not know that failure can hurt, or even that you can fail. This brand of unknowingness lets you take incredible risks onstage without appearing to consider the consequences.

These are the broad sweeping strokes of a dancer's skill set. How would you assemble your own? What do you have, what do you need, and what can you do to develop the skills you don't have?

24 Play Twenty Questions

Thoroughness, like discipline, is one of the most valuable skills. The patience to accumulate detail keeps you grounded and sharp.

Leonardo da Vinci's notebooks are evidence of obsessive thoroughness. For example, Leonardo was fascinated by water. In one section of his notebooks he lists the various aspects of rivers and currents he intended to study:

Of the different rates of speed of currents from the surface of the water to the bottom.

Of the different cross slants between the surface and the bottom.

Of the different currents on the surface of the waters.

Of the different currents on the bed of the rivers.

Of the different depths of the rivers.

Of the different shapes of the hills covered by the waters.

Of the different shapes of the hills uncovered by the waters.

Where the water is swift at the bottom and not above.

Where the water is slow at the bottom and swift above.

Where it is slow below and above and swift in the middle.

Where the water in the rivers stretches itself out and where it contracts. Where it bends and where it straightens itself.

Where it penetrates evenly in the expanses of rivers and where unevenly. Where it is low in the middle and high at the sides.

Where it is high in the middle and low at the sides.

Where the current goes straight in the middle of the stream. Where the current winds, throwing itself on different sides.

Of the different slants in the descents of the water.

By the time Leonardo had considered all of these aspects, he understood rivers and was ready to make any creative use of their power and potential that might occur to him, whatever the context. Asking the question assigned him the task of finding the answer.

Before you approach a topic, write down twenty things you want to know about it. Let's say you've decided to paint a landscape. Here are twenty questions to consider:

1. From what direction is the light coming?
2. What is the elevation?
3. What trees are native to the area?
4. Where is the nearest source of water?
5. What animals are likely to be in view?
6. What season is it?
7. What's the weather?
8. Are you looking down, across, or up?
9. What crops are being cultivated, if any?
10. Are there towns or villages or cities in view?
11. Why are you there?
12. What is attractive about the setting?
13. Is the wind blowing?
14. How much sky can you see?
15. What's behind you that might affect the view?
16. What color predominates in your mind's eye?
17. How many shades of that color do you see in the region?
18. Are other people a part of the image? Who?
19. Are you imagining it today, or at some past or future time?
20. What is the frame of the image?

You may have a totally different set of questions. A portrait will lead to an entirely different set. So will a sculpture, a short story, a short film, a work based in movement.

The asking of the questions, however, sets you the task of learning as much as you can before you start putting paint to canvas, chisel to stone, finger to keyboard. And this questioning process doesn't stop once you've begun. The more you know, the better you can *imagine.*

177

25 Package Your Time

Of all my skills, none is more important than the ability to organize my time. Like many people, I worry on every project that I won't have enough time to do my best. I worry when I have to rely on other people's timetables, that their priorities will collide with mine or, worse, that they don't have any priorities at all, that they're reckless with deadlines. The thought that I will run out of time on a project terrifies me. So I look at the calendar and try to work it all out.

To some this is basic planning: Determine how much time you need versus how much time you have and plan accordingly. But one of the virtues of the creative life is supposed to be that it's open-ended. There's no deadline on a painting or a poem; it's done when it's done. To quote D. W. Harding, "The most important thing is not what the author or artist had in mind to begin with but at what point he decided to stop."

In the collaborative arts—film, theater, choreography among them—we don't have that luxury. Even if there's no set date for a ballet's premiere, I still have to work around the dancers' schedules (and the composer's, and the set designer's, and the lighting director's, and the theater's, too). I still have those dancers coming to the studio as scheduled expecting something wonderful from me. That responsibility weighs on me, and when it's compounded by multiple projects it can be crushing.

I maintain control of the process by envisioning all of my projects as circles within circles on a piece of paper with their deadlines scrawled within the borders of each. Each circle is a self-contained unit, separate, distinct, isolated—like the popular Russian nesting dolls—but each rubs up against and enfolds the other circles, too. After all, if I'm working on several things at once, they inevitably compete with one another. They clamor not only for my time but for my undivided attention.

If I follow my circles and match things up with my calendar, the progression begins to make sense. I look at the concentric circles and tell myself, "I can do this." This routine bolsters my faith in myself. Which instills confidence. Which provides momentum.

Most creative endeavors don't allow precise planning, but it's still vital to have some sense of how long something is going to take you. One successful commercial writer advises people beginning their first novels to allow a year to create a first draft, writing a page a day, and another year to make it good. At first glance, the thought of investing two years in a project is daunting, but a page a day is a manageable output. Also, it's nice to know you're accumulating a *first* draft. You'll get to fix it later.

Think of all the things you want to accomplish in the next few months. How much do they overlap? Do they conflict? Draw your own circles. Make the circles big or little depending on the importance of the task. Use this method for prioritizing your time. Any approach that renews your self-confidence and keeps you moving forward is worth cultivating and repeating.

26 Take Away a Skill

Take away a skill, a vital one. Would you still be able to create? How would you overcome the loss? How would you compensate? What skill would come to the fore to rescue your work?

Business executives run through this type of hypothetical exercise all the time as a way to establish their organization's strengths and preparedness. They're always imagining what-if scenarios in which the company loses something. For example, "What if we lost Executive X to the competition? What would happen to his clients and customers? Would they stay with us or go with him? What are we prepared to do about that?" These are useful because they reveal the powers the company has in reserve. It raises the question, of course, as to why these capabilities have been held back in the first place. But that's the value of thinking hypothetically: It unleashes new talents.

It also forces you to face reality. Jack Welch, when he became CEO of General Electric, had one of his first meetings with the people who ran the company's nuclear reactor business. The executives were forecasting growth in the division based on sales of three or four very expensive nuclear reactors a year. Welch didn't see it that way. Politicians and citizens were losing their enthusiasm for nuclear power; demand for more plants was vanishing. He told his executives, "You're not facing reality. You're running this business as if you have customers for your reactors. You don't. The customers don't exist." He forced them to come up with a plan for a business that doesn't build and sell new reactors but rather services the ones they had already built and sold. He forced them to create a new service business that dealt with the facts as they were, not as they wanted them to be. That's valuable thinking: *Take away new customers. What have you got left?*

This happened to me, not hypothetically, when I broke my ankle working on the Milos Forman film of *Hair.* It was the first time in my life that I had lost my mobility, the first time that I would have to create dance in some manner other than on my body. It was the first time that I wouldn't be able to *show* the dancers what I wanted but rather would have to *tell* them. That's a huge difference for a choreographer. I managed to get through it; for eight weeks I went into the studio and forced myself to visualize what I wanted and then translate it into language that the dancers would understand. I didn't enjoy it, but I discovered two new skills: One, I could verbalize my ideas better than I'd thought I could. Two, I had a talent for refusing to be defeated by reality.

In this regard, my heroes are those who've prevailed over far greater losses than I've ever had to face.

Henri Matisse was bedridden in his home in the south of France with only the use of his arms and imagination in his final years. But he wasn't going to stop working. His mind wouldn't rest. So he came up with a new way of working: paper cutouts. These exquisitely pure creations, out of the most childlike material, are some of my favorite works by Matisse. They are the essence of his art. I doubt he would have ever made them if some of his other skills had not been taken away.

Alicia Alonzo, the great Cuban dancer, was blind for much of her career, but she still performed well into her seventies (the age is just as remarkable as the lack of sight). She could always tell where she was onstage by feeling the heat from the stage lights.

The giant in this category of course is Beethoven, who composed many of his greatest works after he lost his hearing. Freed from the distractions of the new, he reconnected with the ideas and themes that had moved him in his youth, to mine the richness of his classical heritage. We can take great inspiration from this.

Pick one of your skills from the list you made in "Take Inventory of Your Skills" (page 174). Now remove it. What's left? What can you accomplish without it? What does it say about your work habits, your art, your potential?

And if you can do without it, why haven't you?

Chapter 10

ruts and

grooves

It's going to happen sometimes: Despite all the good habits you've developed, the preparation rituals, the organizational tools, the techniques for scratching out pre-ideas and actual ideas, there will come a time when your creativity fails you. You stare at the canvas, the screen, the keyboard, the empty room—and it refuses to meet your eyes. It looks away as if it's ashamed of you. You may as well be painting on shards of broken glass. Your screen shows nothing but wavy lines. Your fingers slip off the keyboard, never getting traction. The room turns dark and cold, and someone is locking the door behind you.

You are in a rut.

When I'm working, I'm always monitoring my momentum, always asking, "Is this piece moving forward or staying in place? Am I in a rut or a groove?" A rut is when you're spinning your wheels and staying in place; the only progress you make is in digging yourself a deeper rut. A groove is different: The wheels turn and you move forward effortlessly. It can mean all the difference in the world.

Let's be clear about what is and is not a rut. A rut is not writer's block (or any other creative block). When you're in a rut, at least you know your motor is running. Writer's block means your engine has shut down and the tank is empty. Being blocked is most often a failure of nerve, with only one solution: *Do something—anything.*

A rut is more like a false start. The engine's kicked over, you've picked your destination, and you're moving. A rut is the part of the journey where you're spinning your wheels, spitting out mud behind you, splattering other people, and not going anywhere. You know you're in a rut when you annoy other people, bore your collaborators and supporters, fail to challenge yourself, and get the feeling that the world is moving on while you're standing still. You may also feel that you've been here before; déjà vu, with some flop sweat on the side, is a sure sign of a rut. Perhaps the surest sign is a feeling of frustration and relief when you're done ("Boy, I'm glad that's over!") rather than anticipatory pleasure ("I can't wait to get back here tomorrow.").

Ruts form for all sorts of reasons.

A rut can be the consequence of a **bad idea.** You shouldn't have started the project in the first place.

A rut can be the end product of **bad timing**. For some reason you are out of sync with the world. You can have the brightest vision with the most mind-blowing idea, but if the world isn't ready for it you can spin your wheels for years.

A rut can form because of **bad luck** or circumstances conspiring against you.

More often than not, I've found, a rut is the consequence of **sticking to tried and tested methods** that don't take into account how you or the world has changed. It's like your mother serving you the same breakfast you loved as a child. You push the meal away half-eaten and she says, "But you always loved Cocoa Puffs and pork sausage." That was then, this is now.

Variations on this theme occur in all aspects of your life. It's staffers at a company walking glumly into the 3:00 P.M. Tuesday meeting long after the weekly gathering has lost its reason for being. That's meeting rut. A shrewd manager will notice the dispirited group, ask "Does anybody want to be here?," and cancel the meeting until further notice.

It's a salesperson sticking with the same sales pitch or a company clinging to its advertising approach long after their customers have changed their buying habits. That's selling rut. You either change the pitch or find new customers.

It's a family going on the same summer vacation year after year, even after the kids have grown and developed other interests: That's vacation rut. There's a lot to be said for tradition, but there's a lot to be said for examining it, too. If the trip bores some of the interested parties, alert parents test out a new vacation— or let the kids stay home.

"We've always done it this way" is not a good enough reason to keep doing it if it isn't working. When an otherwise smart habit or ritual loses its potency and you continue doing it, you're in a rut.

I noticed this when my improvising in the studio began having a curious effect on my dancers. More and more of our rehearsals were routine and dull, going nowhere. The danger and excitement had faded. That's rehearsal rut.

Eventually I realized it was me, not them. When I was young I would work out my ideas on myself for an hour or two each morning before the dancers showed up. Then I'd try my ideas on them. That's fine when you're thirty-five years old and in the best shape of your life; you can blast away on the dance floor for three or four hours every day, and something good will certainly come out of it. But it doesn't work as well twenty years later. It slowly dawned on me that my body wasn't as prolific as it used to be. In my fifties, I had either shed some power or, to put it another way, acquired physical limitations. The range of my movements shrunk. My stamina was diminished. As a result, the ideas I developed on my body no longer challenged my dancers. They were professionals, of course, so they'd do what I asked them to do, but I could see a desultory attitude creeping into the ease with which they tossed off the steps. That's not the effect I'm after; I want my dancers to grab my ideas and abandon common sense. I want them to give something of their own and to push everything to the edge.

So I changed my work habits. I brought in young talented assistants and talked more, danced less. I don't want to paint a picture of myself as an invalid who can't put three steps together without sagging into a heap on the floor. I still improvise alone before rehearsal, but I no longer look to create primarily from my steps. It's a transition any physical director of a certain age has to make—from being a demonstrator to becoming an instructor. I'm not going to lie to you; it *hurts* to come to that realization. I became a choreographer because I longed to dance, and nobody was making the kinds of dances I felt inside me. It was brutal to recognize that my body could no longer take me where my mind wanted to go. But I surely owed it to my dancers to turn onto myself the same brutal honesty with which I viewed their efforts. You can't make this kind of transition if you don't see the need for it, and you won't see the need if you don't analyze all your work habits. When you're in a rut, you have to question everything except your ability to get out of it.

Dealing with ruts is a three-step process of seeing, believing, and repairing.

First, *you have to see the rut.*

If you're like me, you might not always know you're in a rut until it's too late. This is particularly true when you're creating on your own (at least I have the benefit of dancers giving me daily feedback, letting me know when things aren't working). You may be humming along with your novel, writing every day, and then twelve months later you find you have four hundred pages that do not make sense. You have to make a habit of reviewing your efforts along the way, seeing where you've been and where you are to make sure you're still heading in the right direction, if any.

Second, *admit you're in a rut.*

This is harder than it sounds. It requires an admission that you've made a mistake. People don't always do that. They'll even deny that they're in denial. Think about the last time your talents failed you on a project. Did you step back and admit it? Did you pause and wait for a better day? Or did you commit the creative equivalent of throwing good money after bad, trying to tough it out, hoping that time and sheer effort would pay off? It's a harsh thing to do, and a bit ironic: The more disciplined you are, the less you'll be willing to cut your losses and stop the insanity. Truth is, all you're doing is deepening your rut.

The third step is
getting out of the rut.

This is the hard part. Knowing and admitting a problem are not the same as solving
it. But executing a solution is also the fun
part, because the solution saves you and
gets you moving again.

When optimism turns to pessimism during the creative process, you are in a
serious, dangerous rut. So serious that it can become the mother rut—depres-
sion. Forget spinning your wheels; the wheels have come off the wagon. Some
people work their way out of it. Some people take a rest. Some people need the
help of a doctor. I don't have the cure for this one.

Often, it's not the work alone that triggers the shift to pessimism. It can easily be something around you, too. Think: What's happened? Is it trouble with a
spouse or partner? Money? Health? The evening news? Distractions? The

weather? What's making you hate the material you're producing? If it's something in your environment, the simplest solution is change your environment. If it's a micro-rut, a momentary stall as you try to get from one part to another during the day's work, change your scenery. Get out of the house. Stare at the sky. Grab a hoe and tend to your garden. Take a walk. Grab lunch with a friend. Call it a day. Do something that gets you out of the vehicle with the spinning wheels.

One time, after a particularly grueling day of business heartbreaks and creative headaches, I built a fire in my living room fireplace. As I've said, I take great comfort and solace in heat. Heat is practically a sacrament for me, and watching a fire is one of life's miraculous pleasures. Fire has fabulous movement and spatial invention. It is constantly altering, never repeating itself. The flame changes shape, color, height, and depth. Tinker with the fire by adding a log and it veers off at different angles, sometimes swelling into a vertical pyre, other times collapsing into a horizontal twinkle.

The fire show kept me busy for two hours as the day turned into night. I was enveloped in a world of flickering light and thermal pleasure. Campfires have always encouraged the telling of stories, and I began to tell stories to myself. Answers to work problems began to march out of the flames, saying, "Try this beginning and then try this one next." Then I lit candles to enrich the sacrament; I would have released fireflies if they were to be found.

Next I ran a hot bath. Martha Graham liked to boast that she had done her floor series on the shores of all the world's oceans; when I knew her late in her life, she was very arthritic and soaked in hot Epsom salts every day before coming to the studio. Alone in the tub, in another medium of exquisite heat, I began to relax, breathe easily, lose track of time, and shelter myself from invasive ideas. I was where I needed to be, on my way to becoming a complete blank.

Leonardo da Vinci said, "Where there is heat there is life." That vitality is the luxurious reward that heat provides me. Unlike most luxuries, though, it is abundant and virtually free. In its embrace, particularly after a day of despondency, I feel capable of anything.

If you find yourself caught in a bigger rut, what you really need is a new idea, and the way to get it is by giving yourself an aggressive quota for ideas. A tough manager will have realistic quotas for his employees that he keeps to himself and aggressive "stretch" quotas, anywhere from ten percent higher to a lot more, which he imposes on his staff. If his people miss the stretch numbers but exceed the realistic goals, he's happy. If he's a superb manager, he knows how far they can stretch without breaking.

I conduct an exercise along these lines when I lecture at colleges. I'll go backstage and come back with a found object. The last time I did this I returned with a wooden stool. Then I gave the audience a challenge: You've got two minutes to come up with sixty uses for the stool.

A lot of interesting things happen when you set an aggressive quota, even with ideas. People's competitive juices are stirred. Instead of panicking they focus, and with that comes an increased fluency and agility of mind.

People are also forced to suspend critical thinking. To meet the quota, they put their internal critic on hold and let everything out. They're no longer choking off good impulses.

The most interesting thing I've noticed is that there's a consistent order to the quality of ideas. You'd think the sixtieth idea would be the most lame, but for my purposes, which are to trigger leaps of imagination, it's often the opposite. To meet the quota, people begin by listing the most obvious uses for a stool, such as sitting on it, standing on it, or burning it as fuel. These are the least original ideas. After that come the more imaginative uses—a doorstop, an anchor, a weapon, a projectile in a riot, as raw material for sculpture, as a surface to drum on. Then the final ideas come straggling in—as a surface for gymnastics, as a tool for taming lions, as a dancing partner. The closer they get to the sixtieth idea, the more imaginative they become—because they have been forced to stretch their thinking. It's the same arc every time: the first third of the ideas are obvious; the second third are more interesting; the final third show flair, insight, curiosity, even complexity, as later thinking builds on earlier thinking. When you start with a stool, it's easy to think of a chair; only after you see the chair can you think about it as a protective barrier between you and a lion. (I'm not knocking first ideas. They're often the best. But they're rarely the most radical stretch, and that's the purpose of this exercise.)

I don't have to beat the audience over the head with the stool. They get the point: We get into ruts when we run with the first idea that pops into our head, not the last one.

I've been doing this in real life for years in the studio. When I improvise alone or with a dancer to develop ideas for movement, I videotape the entire session. I want *all* of the session's ideas—good, bad, and ridiculous—captured without a filter. The only judgment imposed is whatever self-censoring my partner and I have placed on ourselves, and that's minimal, because we know we're there to improvise and develop freely without restrictions. A three-hour session sets an implicit quota of three hours' worth of ideas.

At day's end, I go through all three hours of tape, searching for a scrap of interesting movement that I've never seen before. If I find thirty seconds of movement out of the three hours, I'm happy. Interestingly, like the stool exercise, the useful ideas tend to come at the end of the session, when we're warmed up and have run through all the obvious steps. It never fails. But that doesn't mean I fast forward to the end. The process of getting to the good stuff is valuable, too. In fact, it's absolutely necessary. Sometimes you can't identify a good idea until you've considered and discarded the bad ones.

This method is no different from a painter running through sketch after sketch until he gets something he likes. His studio floor is littered with crumpled sheets of rejected drawings. It's a lawn of false starts and mediocre solutions, but it is not a lawn of failure. The crumpled sheets are the cost of getting it right. In effect, the artist is running through his quota of sixty ideas for a sketch, only he doesn't know he has a quota.

Challenging your assumptions is another important corrective procedure.

If your car is in a rut, the first thing you do is put it in reverse to see if that provides better traction. Why not do the same to a stalled concept? Part of the excitement of creativity is the headlong rush into action when we latch onto a new idea. Yet, in the excitement, we often forget to apply pressure to the idea, poke it, challenge it, push it around, see if it stands up. Without that challenge, you never know how far astray your assumptions may have taken you.

I remember touring with my dance company in a van in the Midwest years ago. It was late in the afternoon, we were behind schedule and rushing to get to a performance at a college 250 miles north of Davenport, Iowa. We loaded the van, piled in, and somehow found the highway. About 30 miles into the trip, surrounded by flat farmland and no significant landmarks, one of the dancers sitting on the right side of the van looked up and basked in the beautiful setting sun. Then she said, "If we're going north, shouldn't the sun be on our left side?" We were going the wrong way.

Even though the evidence is staring you in the face, you don't always read the evidence correctly—or even bother to think about it.

If you're in a creative rut, the easiest way to challenge assumptions is to switch things around them and make the switch work. The process goes like this:

1. Identify the concept that isn't working.
2. Write down your assumptions about it.
3. Challenge the assumptions.
4. Act on the challenge.

When Paul Newman first met the producers of *Butch Cassidy and the Sundance Kid*, the producers wanted him for the role of Sundance. Newman told them he was much more interested in the Butch role. There was a pause in the room, everyone looked at one another, lightbulbs went off in their heads, and then they all said, "Of course. You're Butch." And that's how Robert Redford was cast as the other guy.

Newman challenged the producers' assumptions by reversing them. You won't always have an outside agent in the person of a powerful star helping you reverse your way out of a rut. Most of the time you have to do it on your own. But this kind of thinking can save you.

(It's fitting that challenging assumptions makes lightbulbs go off in people's heads. The lightbulb was invented by Thomas Edison largely by challenging assumptions and ignoring—or at least tormenting—received wisdom. Lacking any formal education, which he considered his "blessing," Edison approached ideas or experiences with both enthusiasm and skepticism. Edison was the master of challenging assumptions. He systematized this in his notebooks and he tested everything, including employees. Before Edison hired a research assistant, he would invite the candidate over to his lab for a bowl of soup; if the candidate seasoned the soup before tasting it, Edison would not hire the individual. He did not want people who had built so many assumptions into their everyday lives that they assumed the soup wasn't properly seasoned. He wanted fresh minds that would make no assumptions, with an openness that allows ideas to wander in.)

As the Paul Newman story suggests, in the performing arts, casting is one of the assumptions that needs to be challenged violently but often isn't. Theater lore is rife with tales of great scripts, great plays, great films bogged down or even ruined by poor casting. I can see how it happens. Casting is one of the few creative choices where the material you're working with—that is, a real-life human being—has opinions and can talk back to you. If you're writing a novel, your characters are lifeless until you breathe life into them, and even then they don't walk into your studio complaining about their role, their dialogue, or the number of pages you've accorded them in the book. It's the same with paints and marble and notes on a musical score; they don't fight back. But in the theatrical arts, where human emotions are involved, muddled reasoning can creep into your decision making. You yield to the performers' wishes against your better judgment. *This role will make me. I need this role. You owe me more time on stage as a reward for my loyalty and hard work.* These are all legitimate but softheaded thoughts. When the work starts to misfire, you have to get hardheaded about your views.

Sometimes a dancer is wrong for the part, so I recast it with a dancer who is a polar opposite. Sometimes there are too many dancers on stage, confusing the piece, overwhelming the music, or threatening to run into one another onstage—and I have to cut a dancer or two out of the piece or blend several of them into one role. In each case, someone's feelings are hurt—and worse, he's out of a job. It's never an easy decision, but when your work is at stake, you have to be willing to turn everything upside down, damn the human cost.

I even think this way when it's not my creation. If I find myself looking at my watch during a performance—meaning I'm disengaged, the creators and performers have lost my attention, when is this over?—I'll entertain myself by changing and editing the work. What if Actresses A and B switched roles? What if Scene 4 became Scene 1, kicking off the piece rather than showing up too late? What if the ballerina entered from the back and crossed the stage on a diagonal, which might be more compelling to the eye? What if that tall kid in the corps were her partner instead of the fellow who doesn't look as if he enjoys dancing with her? I don't do this to be mean-spirited. I'm well aware of the compromises that have to be made with every production. But it's a good exercise. I'm challenging the assumptions. It sharpens my rut-fighting skills.

This mental exercise serves double duty. It not only gets me out of a rut, it sharpens my show-doctoring skills for when I really need them. I learned this from Jerry Robbins, a true man of the theater, who made a point of going to see everything because he could find something useful in even the worst productions. He'd sit there, viewing the catastrophe onstage, and imagine how he would have done it differently. A bad evening at the theater for everyone else was a creative workout for him. It's one way he honed the skills that made him one of the greatest show doctors of all time.

These are some methods to get you out of a rut, to help you regain momentum as you work. The ultimate goal is to find what I call, for lack of a better term, your groove.

Getting out of a rut is different from creating a groove. It's the difference between knowing a bad idea (and avoiding it) and coming up with a good idea. They are not the same thing.

When you're in a groove, you're not spinning your wheels; you're moving forward in a straight and narrow path without pauses or hitches. You're unwavering, undeviating, and unparalleled in your purpose. A groove is the best place in the world. It's where I strive to be, because when you're in it you have the freedom to explore, where everything you question leads you to new avenues and new routes, everything you touch miraculously touches something else and transforms it for the better. When you rise in the morning, you know exactly what you're doing that day. When I think of a groove, I imagine Bach bounding out of bed to compose his preludes and fugues, knowing that he had twenty-four keys to work with. "Let's see," he must have thought, "today I'll tackle G sharp major and A flat minor." A groove is a great comfort.

The funny thing about a groove is that you rarely know you're in it until you fall out. My groove is like what athletes call being "in the zone." Every pass finds the receiver. Every jump shot hits nothing but net. The pitcher's best curveball looks as big as a volleyball as you smack it for a hit. You see the snaking twenty-five-foot putt going into the hole, and it accedes to your wishes, rolling into the cup as if it were on rails.

It's the reason batters have hitting streaks, pitchers toss perfect games, basketball players light up the scoreboard for sixty points, and runners shatter world records. It's the sweet spot in time when everything is in sync and nothing misfires. And then it's over. Tiger Woods misses putts. Michael Jordan's jump shot goes cold. There's no point in analyzing it. If you could figure out how you get into a groove you could figure out how to maintain it. That's not going to happen. The best you can hope for is the wisdom and good fortune to occasionally fall into a groove.

Grooves come in all shapes and sizes, and they're usually preceded by a breakthrough idea, also in all shapes and sizes.

There are mini-grooves that last a morning or an afternoon. You sit down at the piano and a complete tune pours out of you. The breakthrough is usually emotional, not technical. It could be something as minor as hearing some good news, or meeting a sexy, flirtatious person the night before, or having a good breakfast. But just like a piece of good news or a good breakfast, the feeling fades. The next morning it's not the same. The groove is gone.

There are grooves where everything flows for days, weeks, months, and you knock out a finished work in record time. The novelist Mark Salzman tells of all the agonizing missteps that led him to waste five years trying to write a follow-up to his first novel, *The Soloist*. When he reread the new manuscript, he realized it was bad and, as he told Lawrence Weschler in the *New Yorker*, he was "destroyed." His wife suggested that a change of scenery in the form of a five-week stay at a New England artists' retreat would do him good. "I went," he says, "though without any particular intention of writing; that book had hurt me enough. I just wanted to exist as if in a kind of Zen retreat.

"And you know what? It was like waking from a bad dream. All of a sudden, everything was like a gift: the fall colors, the sounds, the little homemade cookies in the picnic baskets. But mainly the removal of all the reminders of art as a profession, as a way of making money or gaining a reputation and the like. Rather, here I was in a community of people who seemed dedicated to art almost like a sacred pursuit."

Salzman's novel is set in a Carmelite cloister and tells the story of a nun who suddenly and mysteriously matures as a poet. In midlife she is blessed with a radiance that feeds her creative outpourings and brings her closer to God. The cause, it turns out, is a brain tumor, which is operable. Her spiritual crisis is whether to have the tumor removed and return to her dull existence without death hovering, or to revel in the grace and beauty that has entered her life, even as it costs her that life. It's a novel about a woman in a groove, albeit a terminal one.

The combination of story, change of scenery, and Salzman's torment provided him with a breakthrough. "Suddenly, sitting there in my cabin," he says, "I realized that all along I'd been living my nun's life myself. And, once I saw that, the book wrote itself in five weeks, with me in a state that I can only describe as euphoric. The words were coming to me with labels attached: 'Put me next to him.' And when it was done, the way I felt about that book made everything that had come before worthwhile."

I love happy endings, and Salzman's tale is proof that grooves exist and can, with luck and pluck, be self-induced.

There also are mega-grooves, long stretches of time when piece after piece comes out of you with satisfying results. You don't realize you're in this state until you're too far along or it's gone, but it often starts with a mega-breakthrough.

Many creative thinkers have had an epiphanic moment where they make a quantum leap forward in ability and vision. It may not be obvious to the untrained eye, but you know it and it shows in your work.

One for me happened in 1969. I was married, twenty-eight years old, and living in upstate New York. I was unassailed by distractions: no artificially imposed schedules, no meetings, no inconvenient commuting. The phone did not ring for days. Like Salzman, I was in an artist's retreat, only it was a decrepit farm that my husband and I worked. Everything was efficient, focused, with purpose. When I rowed a boat, kneaded bread, or mowed the grass, I felt linked to ancient physical chores. Everything from sweeping out corners to thinking about how a compost heap works informed my creative efforts. It was the year of the Woodstock festival, which took place just over the mountains from the farm. It was the year the New York Mets won the World Series. I listened to the games devoutly on the kitchen radio, and even Tom Seaver's pitching motion found its way into a dance called *The One Hundreds.* I made more dance that summer than I ever have.

My breakthrough arrived in a piece called *The Fugue,* which was a set of twenty variations on a twenty-count theme for three dancers that I took from the fugal structure of Bach's *A Musical Offering.* Mind you, I didn't actually use Bach's music (*The Fugue* is performed in silence); I was still a rustic who couldn't afford music, live or recorded. Plus, I wanted my dances to stand on their own feet, without the support of anyone's music. (As ever, it was all about self-reliance.) But in studying the score and imagining how it translated into dance, I began to see the logic in Bach's majestic notes, how he would take a phrase and reverse it, or invert it, or switch it from the right hand to the left, or reverse the inversion. It struck me that, given the symmetry of the human body and how its joints function, you could do the same thing with dance steps. Take three steps forward (that's one move). Take three steps backwards (that's another). Now take those three steps to your left, then your right (that's two more moves). Now switch everything to the other foot. Now run it backwards, or more accurately in retrograde, like film running backwards through a projector (I imagined milk being sucked back into a bottle after being poured). Now turn the body ninety degrees to the right or left to face a new front. Now add rhythmic alterations so that all these phrases can be done in the original tempo, in double time, or in half time. Now insert a quick arbitrary movement, say three fast hand claps, into one of the basic phrases (I called this "stuffing"). Now take these moves on one person and add a second dancer, and a third, each making canonic entrances two counts after the other (think of "Row, Row, Row Your Boat" and how everyone enters fixed beats after one another).

It gets complicated, but in devising *The Fugue,* one variation a day—outdoors in the pasture on sunny days, indoors when it rained—I discovered I had given myself a completely new way of handling movement. Reversal, inversion, retrograde, retrograded inversion, stuffing, canon, and so on. It was a vocabulary sufficiently rich with possibilities and variations that I would be using and building on it for the rest of my life.

I didn't know if other choreographers knew this like the back of their hand and had never bothered to tell me, but it was a revelation to me. It was as if I had been painting with black, white, and red and someone said, "Twyla, have you heard of the color blue? And green? And yellow? And all the shades of the spectrum in between?"

I could finally speak. I didn't realize then that this was a choreographic language for the rest of my life, but I sensed it was a breakthrough.

Within a year of *The Fugue*'s premiere in August 1970, I was mounting new dances like *Eight Jelly Rolls* in New York City—with, for the first time, music, and Jelly Roll Morton no less! In short order, I made *The Bix Pieces,* to the jazz of Bix Beiderbecke, and *The Raggedy Dances* to Scott Joplin and Mozart, and *Deuce Coupe* to the songs of the Beach Boys. They are all pieces that endure and please me. They slide into one another, sharing a beautiful groove of rhythm and language and intention. They make sense taken together. They look inevitable.

You only appreciate a groove in hindsight. It's hard even to notice it when you're in the middle of it. You don't congratulate yourself and say "I'm in a groove." With a mega-groove like the one I was in, all you feel is *This is what creating is like for me now.* You know that you're learning and growing and stretching and being at your best. You don't know how long it's going to last. All you can do is accept it with gratitude and try not to screw it up.

Eventually the groove shut down and became stalled in a rut. My marriage broke up and my personal life began insinuating itself into the spines and stories of my dances. I veered away—as anyone eventually would—from the exquisite musical groove that jazz and popular music provided and tried my hand at other musical sources such as symphonies and works by my contemporaries. An unsettling period ensued for six or seven years in the 1970s. It wasn't exactly a rut—some of my "greatest hits" like *Sue's Leg* and *Push Comes to Shove* came during this period—but you could say it was grooveless. In hindsight, I think it happened because I had started doing more freelance projects outside my own company; I had left my home base, a big source of my groove. In 1979, when I returned to the home base of my own repertory company, I also returned to the classic jazz of Willie "the Lion" Smith for *Bakers Dozen* and, once again, I felt regrooved with the spirit of my first jazz dances.

I mention this because there's a lesson here about finding your groove. Yes, you can find it via a breakthrough in your craft. But you can also find it through other means—in congenial material, in a perfect partner, in a favorite character or comfortable subject matter.

In my early jazz pieces, I found my groove in the grooves created by others. The jazz masters had a style that was congenial to me. Material that feels compatible can lead you right into a whole new groove.

You can also find a groove in a perfect partner. Witness Mozart and his three Da Ponte operas, *Don Giovanni, The Marriage of Figaro,* and *Così fan tutte.* Mozart, perhaps more than anyone ever, made his own grooves, but he surely found something congenial in the brilliant librettos of Lorenzo Da Ponte. Mozart wrote other great operas, but those three are miraculous. He found his groove in a collaborator.

John Updike seems to find his novelistic groove in the character of Rabbit Angstrom. His nearly twenty novels vary in quality, but the four devoted to this single character—*Rabbit, Run; Rabbit Redux; Rabbit Is Rich;* and *Rabbit at Rest*—seem to provide a booster rocket even to Updike's considerable powers.

Rembrandt found his best subject in himself. Throughout his career he painted, etched, and sketched self-portraits. The genre of self-portrait was a groove for him. It was comfortable—and convenient. After all, he was always available when he needed a model.

In the end, ruts and grooves are different sides of the same coin. The work itself will tell you which side you're looking at. Does it give you pleasure or pain? You must try to escape the ruts and create the grooves.

The call to a creative life is not supposed to be torture. Yes, it's hard work and you have to make sacrifices. Yes, it's a noble calling; you're volunteering in an army of sorts, alongside a phalanx of artists who have preceded you, many of whom are your mentors and guides, upon whose work you build, without whom you have no fixed points of reference. They form a tradition that you have implicitly sworn to protect, even while you aim to refashion it and sometimes even shatter it.

But it's also supposed to be fun.

My rituals and preparations and "weeks without" might make the creative life sound like a tough stretch on Parris Island. That is not what it's like at all. I look forward to the moment the dancers walk into the studio, and I miss them immediately when they go for the day. I regard all the great composers who give me music to dance to as my *inamorati*. I get a thrill akin to scoring a touchdown when a dancer takes a difficult move and absolutely nails it—and then takes it a step or two beyond what I had even imagined. At moments like that, if I had a ball, I would spike it on the studio floor.

exercises

27 Do a Verb

Of all the exercises that help me when I'm at a creative dead end, my favorite is "Do a Verb." All it means is that I pick a verb and act it out physically. For example, the verb "squirm" may get me wiggling my hips, shrugging my shoulders, and contorting my limbs in such a way that I'm forced to extend it into a complete dance phrase. I could do the same for "dart" or "twirl" or "chafe" or hundreds of other verbs. As part of the exercise, I videotape myself, and reviewing the tape almost always reveals something strange and new—a tilt of the head, a bend of the elbow, a turn of the ankle—or any new combination of moves—that thrills or surprises and gets me started.

You may not think that doing a verb is practical or productive for anyone but a dancer. I disagree. The chemistry of the body is inseparable from the chemistry of the brain. Movement can stimulate anyone.

I've been conducting "Do a Verb" sessions in my lectures for the past few years. I invite people in the audience to pick ten verbs and then do them onstage. It loosens people up, gets them involved, and gives them something *doable* to do. That's important: An exercise must be doable, not frustrating, if you want it to yield something productive. It must tax you enough that your creative muscles will adapt and get stronger, but not so much that it leads you to abandon the effort. It should present a way of thinking or acting that's different from your usual mode; after all, you're doing the exercise because the usual isn't working for you right now.

For a few months I collected all the verb lists that people handed in and I analyzed them. Not surprisingly, certain verbs appeared no matter where I was or who was in the audience. I call them my Civilian Big Ten: *push, spin, run, jump, twist, roll, skip, turn, walk,* and *fall.* Perhaps I was influencing the audience; if they've come to see me, there's a good chance they're interested in dance and what I do, and these particular verbs reflect what my dancers do onstage. No matter. The verb choices may be predictable and common, but here's the amazing thing: No one who comes up onto the stage ever does these ten verbs exactly the same way. Take, for example, the verb "twist." People twist to the left and they twist to the right. Some twist their neck. Some twist their upper body. Some twist below the waist. Some twist their arms, some twist their fingers, some twist their legs and toes. One fellow twisted his tongue.

It was the same thing with all the other verbs. The most mundane verbs yielded the most uncommon responses. This is a testament to everyone's innate creativity. If you tax yourself, if you force yourself to stretch a little, you will astonish yourself and possibly others. That's reason enough to "Do a Verb."

The best thing about it, though, is that everyone can do it—and discover something about themselves. In Seattle one woman who came up onstage was so shy and nervous and closed-in that she couldn't come up with ten verbs. (Yet she had the nerve to get onstage in front of five hundred people.) So I asked her to start with one verb. She chose "walk," and I suspect she chose it because she believed that anyone can walk, even she. She started walking . . . and walking . . . and walking in the most tedious manner, so tediously in fact that I fretted the audience would walk out on us. I stopped her and told her to change the walk. I showed her that she could perhaps walk backwards. She refused to do that. She continued walking around the stage, tedious as ever . . . and then an idea struck her: "Well," she said, "I can change my rhythm." And her walk changed. "And I could add a turn after five steps," she said.

And she turned. "And I could throw in a hop, and reverse the direction of the turn, and repeat it." It was quite stunning and memorable. Once she realized she could alter the rhythm of her walk, the floodgates of her imagination opened. There onstage in Seattle, the woman was coming very close to creating choreography on herself. The audience gave her a standing ovation.

I admit that, as a choreographer, I have an extreme bias about the untapped power of movement in our creative lives. Movement and physical activity are my materials, but more than that, they're how we stay in touch with our body—and the body is how we stay in touch with the outside world. Anything that puts our instrument through its paces has to improve us, make us sharper, more connected to the world.

Choreography is not the purpose of "Do a Verb." But choosing a word and applying movement to it generates ideas, and one idea begets another, to a point where you achieve a creative momentum that's hard to stop and takes you to places you could never predict. An exercise that lets you discover your potential this way is one you should eagerly come back to day after day.

28 Build a Bridge to the Next Day

The only bad thing about having a good creative day is that it ends, and there's no guarantee we can repeat it tomorrow. One good day does not necessarily beget another. But there are ways to increase the chances of successive successes.

Ernest Hemingway had the nifty trick of always calling it a day at a point when he knew what came next. He built himself a bridge to the next day. I cannot think of a better creative organizational tool. The Hemingway bridge is how you extend a mini-groove.

I try to do a variation on this bridge. I always quit for the day before everyone's totally exhausted. I stop when there's still some energy left in the room and I know where we would have gone if we hadn't stopped. Knowing what comes next is like crocheting: The end of one day knits into the next, and you wind up with a garment that is flexible but strong.

A savvy stand-up comedian always knows to leave the audience begging for more. You should do the same with your work. Don't drive yourself to the point of being totally spent. Try to stop while you have a few drops left in the tank, and use that fuel to build a bridge to the next day.

Some people, if only for sanity and the maintenance of a humane routine, give themselves a creative quota. Painters stop when they fill up a measurable section of canvas, playwrights when they draft out a complete scene, writers when they hit one thousand words or the clock chimes 5:00 P.M. They stop no matter where they are on the canvas or page. I know one writer who gives himself both options: He stops at a set time or when he hits his word quota, whichever comes first. He is religious about this routine. But he connects to the next day with a fixed nighttime routine as well: Just before he falls asleep, he reads the last few sentences he wrote. Without fail, he wakes up the next morning brimming with ideas, sentences, whole paragraphs for the next portion of his story. He claims he flies out of bed sometimes so he can get all the words down before they disappear. Apparently, filling up with words and ideas before sleep gives his tired brain some useful work to do as it regroups and refreshes itself overnight. What his conscious brain can't handle, his subconscious can.

He may be one of those blessed individuals who can compartmentalize his thoughts and turn his creativity on and off at will. But he's on to something useful. In effect, he's letting his subconscious build his bridge for him. That just might work for you, too.

In every situation, at the beginning or end of the workday, you have a choice. You can look back or you can look forward. My advice: look forward. Always think about the next day. Don't go into the studio thinking, "Hmmm, let's see, what was I doing yesterday?" It takes more energy to twist yourself around and look back than it does to face forward.

If you've been following a don't-stop-till-you-drop routine—that is, you only quit when you're totally wiped out—rethink that. This is how ruts form. As an exercise, for the next week or so, end your working day when you still have something in reserve.

Now ask yourself, exactly what is it that you're putting into reserve. Is it raw energy? Is it desire? Is it a few more ideas left unexplored? Is it something you meant to say to someone but didn't? Whatever it is, describe it in writing on a notepad or index card. Put the note away and don't think about it for the rest of the day. Start the next day by looking at your note.

Harry Truman said that whenever he wrote a letter in anger to anyone, he put the letter away in a desk drawer for twenty-four hours, then he reread it to make sure he still felt the way he did when he wrote it. It's the same with your note. When you start the next day with the note, you'll be tapping into that reserve from the day before. If it's true, as John Updike writes, that "each day, we wake slightly altered, and the person we were yesterday is dead," then you will approach the impulse behind the note as a new person. At worst, the note will give you something to start with. More likely, the new you will find a way to improve on it.

With methods like these are grooves formed.

29 Know When to Stop Tinkering

The poet Paul Valéry said, "A poem is never finished, only abandoned."

We all know people who are forever tinkering with their work—editing, refining, redoing, trying to make it perfect (whatever that means!). They don't know when to stop.

Knowing when to stop is almost as critical as knowing how to start. How do you know when something is not only the best that you can do but the best that it can be?

Some people are lucky in having artificial and arbitrary stop signs that put an end to all their fussing. Writers have deadlines. Playwrights have strictly scheduled openings based on theater availability. Filmmakers have fixed premieres. Painters and sculptors have gallery exhibitions. The calendar tells them when they are finished.

It's much trickier when you're working on your own, and for your own reasons.

Think of the messiest room in your house. One day you decide to clear the clutter. How do you know when you're done cleaning and organizing? In theory, the only perfectly clean room is an empty room. But that doesn't stop you from charging into a room, trashing the unwanted items, putting the books back on shelves, folding the clothes neatly into their appropriate drawers, putting the papers in their appropriate files and the pencils and paper clips and floppy disks where they belong. Then you sweep and scrub and dust. If you're really good at this, you have a system for organizing clutter: You allocate resting places for your glasses, keys, wallet, and slippers so you can always find them; you store similar things together; you put things you use most often in the easiest-to-get places; you label boxes so you know what's in them; you arrange your clothes according to color. Eventually you reach a point where you look around and you're satisfied. There are no loose ends. Everything is in its place, put away or accounted for or easily accessed. The room exudes order and harmony. When you look around, you're happy.

That, more or less, is the feeling you get when it's time to stop. There are no loose ends, no clutter, and all the moving parts of the work are in their proper places. There are no more problems that keep you up nights, and the solutions feel elegant and inevitable.

Remember this the next time you wonder if a piece is finished. If you don't have the feeling that you've straightened out a messy room, keep working.

It's a little awkward for me to appreciate this because a dance doesn't stand still, even when you think you've stopped working on it. A book is done when it's published, a film when it's released, a painting when it leaves the artist's studio. A marble sculpture is literally set in stone. But in dance, there is no script to follow and no two performances are alike. The work exists only when it is performed and then repeated; between performances, it disappears. As its creator, I have to constantly monitor the performances to make sure the audience is getting a reasonable facsimile of what I thought I had finished. In this environment, it's hard to say when you've stopped working on a piece.

To force myself to let my creations go, I've developed a ritual that gives me satisfying closure: I name the piece. Attaching a name to the work is always the last thing I do. It's a signal to myself that I finally understand it. As Tracy Kidder wrote in *The Soul of a New Machine,* "Good engineers ship." In other words, while perfection is a wonderful goal, there comes a point where you have to let your creation out into the world or it isn't worth a tinkerer's damn.

30 Brew Ruts into Grooves

A bad habit—that is, one that doesn't produce good results—is a rut. Coffee is a rut for me. I need a cup or two every morning, and I don't know why. Part of it,

I'm sure, is its addictive properties. But I don't enjoy it that much.

At one point, I played a game of delaying my daily coffee until I produced something solid that day. No good work, no good coffee. I transformed coffee from rut to reward. To be honest, this didn't last long. Within a month, I was back into my coffee grind. I don't know. You can't be stoic and strong about everything. Some things in life are just meant to be enjoyed simply because you enjoy them. They are their own rationale.

But the mere act of thinking about my coffee rut had a transformative effect. I now regard coffee in a positive light. It's my coffee groove.

Pick a "bad" habit—whether it's coffee or reading the newspaper in its entirety every day to avoid writing—and do something to make it "good." Realize that you don't need elimination, just moderation, so it's working for you. Exorcise the rut. Exercise the groove.

an "A" in failure

Chapter 11

A math professor at Williams College bases ten percent of his students' grades on failure. Mathematics is all about trying out new ideas—new formulas, theorems, approaches—and knowing that the vast majority of them will be dead ends. To encourage his students not to be afraid of testing their quirkiest ideas in public, he rewards rather than punishes them for coming up with wrong answers.

Every creative person has to learn to deal with failure, because failure, like death and taxes, is inescapable. If Leonardo and Beethoven and Goethe failed on occasion, what makes you think you'll be the exception?

I don't mean to romanticize failure, to parrot the cliché "If you're not failing, you're not taking enough risks," especially if that view "liberates" you to fail too often. Believe me, success is preferable to failure. But there is a therapeutic power to failure. It cleanses. It helps you put aside who you aren't and reminds you who you are. Failure humbles.

The best failures are the private ones you commit in the confines of your room, alone, with no strangers watching. Private failures are great. I encourage you to fail as much as you want in private. It will cost you a little in terms of efficiency—the more you fail, the longer it takes to finish—but no one has to see this. Private failures are the first drafts that get tossed in the wastebasket, the sketches crumpled up on the floor, the manuscripts that stay in the drawer. They are the not-so-good ideas you reject en route to finding the one that clicks.

When I tape a three-hour improvisational session with a dancer and find only thirty seconds of useful material in the tape, I am earning straight A's in failure. Do the math: I have rejected 99.7 percent of my work that day. It would be like a writer knocking out a two-thousand-word chapter and upon re-reading deciding that only three words were worth keeping. Painful, yes, but for me absolutely necessary.

What's so wonderful about wasting that kind of time? It's simple: The more you fail in private, the less you will fail in public. In many ways, the creative act is editing. You're editing out all the lame ideas that won't resonate with the public. It's not pandering. It's exercising your judgment. It's setting the bar a little higher for yourself, and therefore your audience.

If you forget this—if you let down your guard, or lower your standards, or compromise too quickly, or leave in something that should be rejected—you'll have to deal with the other, more painful kind of failure, the public kind.

Some of my favorite dancers at New York City Ballet were the ones who fell the most. I always loved watching Mimi Paul; she took big risks onstage and went down often. Her falls reminded you that the dancers were doing superhuman things onstage, and when she fell, I would realize, "Damn, she's human." And hitting the ground seemed to transform Mimi: It was as though the stage absorbed the energy of her fall and injected it back into her with an extra dose of fearlessness. Mimi would bounce back up, ignore the fall, and right before my eyes would become superhuman again. I thought, "Go Mimi!" She became greater because she had fallen. Failure enlarged her dancing.

That should be your model for dealing with failure.

When you fail in public, you are forcing yourself to learn a whole new set of skills, skills that have nothing to do with creating and everything to do with surviving.

Jerome Robbins liked to say that **you do your best work after your biggest disasters.** For one thing, it's so painful it almost guarantees that you won't make those mistakes again. Also, you have nothing to lose; you've hit bottom, and the only place to go is up. A fiasco compels you to change dramatically. The golfer Bobby Jones said, "I never learned anything from a match I won." He respected defeat and he profited from it.

Failure creates an interesting tug of war between forgetting and remembering. It's vital to be able to forget the pain of failure while retaining the lessons from it. I've always found it easier to put something that wasn't very successful behind me than to move on to something new after an effort that was acclaimed. After a certifiable success, I always think, "I could lose this," and so I cling to it. (For this reason, Duke University basketball coach Mike Krzyzewski banned his teams from calling themselves the "defending national champions," because he felt this made them think defensively. Also, he argued that you only defend something that can be taken away from you, and your past successes will always be yours no matter what.) A part of me hates to let go of success and move on. After a certifiable failure, however, I can't wait to move on. I'm thinking, "Get back to work. Fix it. Do it different and better the next time."

That's the tug of war. You have to forget the failure to get it behind you, but at the same time you have to remember the reasons for it. People accommodate this duality in their own ways. I know one writer who frames all his rejection letters and hangs them up in the guest bathroom for every visitor to see. He scoffs at failure. I know an actress who does the same with her most vicious reviews, mocking those who mock her. That which to anyone else is a loss is to the artist a gain.

My heroes in *The Odyssey* are the older warriors who have been through many wars. They don't hide their scars, they wear them proudly as a kind of armor. When you fail—whether your short film induces yawns or your photographs inspire people to say "That's nice" (ouch!) or your novel is trashed in a journal of opinion that matters to you—the best thing to do is acknowledge your battle scars and gird yourself for the next round. Tell yourself, "This is a deep wound. But it's going to heal and I will remember this wound. When I go back into the fray it will serve me well."

To get the full benefit of failure you have to understand the reasons for it.

First, there's a failure of **skill.** You have an idea in mind but not the requisite skills to pull it off. This is the cruelest, crudest, most predictable form of failure. Your reach exceeds your grasp. In my case, it might involve having an insufficient vocabulary of movement, or not recognizing how the audience will read a particular gesture or move. It's no different for a composer trying to write a fugue without skill in counterpoint, or a writer constructing dialogue with a tin ear for how his characters speak. There's only one solution to this type of failure: *Get to work.* Develop the skills you need.

Then there's a failure of **concept.** You have a weak idea that doesn't hold up under your daily ministrations. You torment the idea, and instead of growing it shrivels up. It could be a bad story idea, bad subject matter, bad casting, bad partners, bad timing. You scramble in the beginning to mask this fundamental error, hoping that maybe through guile and trickery you can redeem the work. But it catches up with you. Sows' ears tend to remain sows' ears. Get out while the getting's good.

A third kind of failure is one of judgment. You leave something in the piece that should have been discarded, left on the cutting room floor. Perhaps you let your guard down for a moment and suspended your usual good judgment. Maybe you let someone else's judgment substitute for yours. Maybe you didn't want to hurt somebody's feelings. The only way to avoid this mistake is to remember at all times that you're the one who'll be judged by the final product. The actor whose scene you want to cut isn't responsible for the whole film; you are. The friend who tells you she likes the five-page description of a squirrel in the park doesn't have her name on the book jacket; you do. It's a hard mistake to avoid when you're starting out, but the sooner you demonstrate good judgment, the sooner people will give you the clout to exercise it.

I don't mess up this way anymore; I'm willing to be regarded as a tyrant to keep my vision intact. I've auditioned 900 dancers in order to hire 4 of them. It takes a certain steeliness of character and an intense dislike of failure to tell 896 people that they are somehow lacking in your eyes. But I don't care if I torture casting agents and scouts and staff; if they send me 100 consecutive dancers who almost intrigue me, but not quite, I'll tell them, "Get me more. Get me different." I'll say I'm sorry for being so ornery, but I'm not really apologizing. Neither should you when it's your judgment on the line.

The worst is failure of nerve. You have everything going for you except the guts to support your idea and explore the concept fully. The corrosive thought that you will look foolish holds you back from telling the truth. I wish I had a cure for this. All I have is the certainty of experience that looking foolish is good for you. It nourishes the spirit. You appreciate this more and more over the years as the need to not look foolish fades with youth. (Remember the centenarian who when asked about the best part of living such a long life replied, "No more peer pressure.")

There's failure through repetition. As a choreographer, I'm constantly forced to revisit my past. Repertory is the bread and butter of a choreographer. You have to repeat yourself to make a living. Painters don't have to get up in the morning and repaint *Starry Night* on commission in order to afford a new canvas; Saul Bellow doesn't have to retype *Henderson the Rain King* in order to get people to read his latest book. But choreographers create a dance, teach it to dancers in rehearsal, watch it being performed, and if it's a success, get to teach it to new dancers so it can be performed again and again and again. It's wonderful that audiences love my old works and want to keep seeing them, but after a while I feel like Bruce Springsteen must when his fans demand to hear "Born to Run" at every concert.

Repetition is a problem if it forces us to cling to our past successes. Constant reminders of the things that worked inhibit us from trying something bold and new. We lose sight of the fact that we weren't searching for a formula when we first did something great; we were in unexplored territory, following our instincts and passions wherever they might lead us. It's only when we look back that we see a path, and it's only there because we blazed it.

After his success with Mickey Mouse, Walt Disney's next huge hit was the cartoon short of "The Three Little Pigs," which became a national phenomenon in 1933. It was billed above the main feature on most theater marquees. Its hit song, "Who's Afraid of the Big Bad Wolf?," became a Depression-era anthem.

Disney's film distributor, United Artists, urged him to cash in on the success of "The Three Little Pigs" with other pig-related cartoons. He resisted at first but was finally persuaded by his brother Roy. None of the three follow-ups— "The Big Bad Wolf," "Three Little Wolves," and "The Practical Pig"—succeeded like the original, leading Walt Disney to conclude, "You can't top pigs with pigs." Once Disney realized that you cannot repeat your successes in the entertainment business, he was free to push the envelope with his first full-length animated feature, the classic *Snow White and the Seven Dwarfs*.

Finally, and most profoundly, there is failure that comes from denial. Creating anything new and fresh is a brazen, presumptuous act. You're assuming that the world cares about what you have to say. You can't afford to be paralyzed by the familiar fears of: What if no one shows up? What if no one likes it? What if I don't measure up? What if they laugh? So you become adept at slipping into denial mode. Anything less and you might never get out of bed in the morning.

But the same mechanism that protects you from your worst fears can blind you to reality. Denial becomes a liability when you see that something is not working and you refuse to deal with it. You tell yourself "I'll fix it later," or you convince yourself that you can get away with it, that your audience won't notice the weak spots. This is bad denial. You won't get very far relying on your audience's ignorance.

Change—changing the work and how we work—is the unpleasant task of *dealing* with that which we have been *denying*. It is probably the biggest test in the creative process, demanding not only an admission that you've made a mistake but that you know how to fix it. It requires you to challenge a status quo of your own making.

The process that led *Movin' Out* to its Broadway success demonstrates so many different types of failure and correction that it's a perfect case study in the art of change. Let's take a look at how many things can go wrong even when you know the pitfalls going in, and how to turn around something as unwieldy as a multimillion-dollar theatrical enterprise.

I've already explained how I conceived the idea of a dance show set to the songs of Billy Joel, and the research and preparation that went into its creation. But that is just a small part of the story.

Mounting an expensive Broadway musical is usually an obstacle course of blind alleys, logjams, and political intrigues. Miraculously, we avoided all that up front. I had the idea, I secured Billy's blessing, and I quickly found enough seed money from a major Broadway producer to hire dancers and a band. A few months later, in October 2001, on a spacious midtown Manhattan soundstage, I unveiled a stripped-down version of the show for Billy, the producers, would-be investors, and friends. No costumes, no set, no lights, not even a name for the show (it was referred to as The Thoel Project); just sixteen dancers and ten musicians performing on a bare studio floor. The audience loved it, and within hours the show was fully invested with an $8.5 million budget.

It went so smoothly I had to pinch myself.

The show continued on that smooth path for the next few months as I auditioned more dancers; hired set, costume, and lighting designers; and assembled the production staff. Rehearsals went swiftly, sets were built, schedules came together, and soon we had an out-of-town opening at the Shubert Theater in Chicago set for July 2002, with a Broadway premiere to follow in October. For the longest time, the biggest headache was deciding what to title the show. Just about every phrase from a Billy Joel song was suggested (with the possible exception of *For the Longest Time*) before we settled on *Movin' Out*. It was a period of high-efficiency productivity. The choreography was coming together (a lot of it having been developed for the workshop production), but there were seeds of doubt already present about some aspects of the show, and the logic of the schedule kept us from looking at a few basic problems (see *denial,* above).

Our show bore little resemblance to the standard musical. There were no characters on stage breaking from dialogue into song. The action wasn't in the songs, it was in the dancing.

But the realities of the marketplace demanded that we call what we were presenting "a musical." When you're charging Broadway theater prices and trying to fill Broadway-sized houses, it makes the money people nervous to call what you're putting up onstage "dance," or, worse, "full-length ballet," even if you can work the word *rock* into the billing. So "a musical" is how we described the show that we first presented in front of a paying audience in Chicago.

There's a long tradition in the American musical theater of trying out Broadway-bound shows in towns like Chicago, Boston, New Haven, and Philadelphia. You do this to smooth out the production kinks, to let the performers find their legs, and to fix anything that doesn't work for the audience. With so much at stake, in an age when a poor opening night review in the *New York Times* can doom a show from the outset, little is left to chance.

I knew the balance between the songs and the staging was still a bit rough, but I hoped the show was strong enough that audiences wouldn't notice (see, again, *denial*). Particularly in some of the early numbers, I was letting Billy's songs tell the story instead of making the dance do it (see *judgment*, above). Billy's songs create wonderful characters, but there's no continuity from one to another—there was never supposed to be. Anthony, for example, in the song "Movin' Out" doesn't interact with Brenda from "Scenes from an Italian Restaurant." Yet in my story they do. I needed to tell my story and not worry about the story being told in the songs. We had recruited a fabulous band and a terrific pair of singers to perform the music. We knew the audience's love of Billy's songs would be a big part of its attraction to the show. We had, we felt, a team that was far better than any conventional musical could possibly present: better singers, and vastly better dancers, than any singer/dancer/actors could be. What we didn't have, however, was a conventional musical, and that was what the audience was expecting.

My worries were confirmed with the first week of preview performances in Chicago. The difficulties were there right from the beginning. They *began* with the beginning. We knew that the biggest name in the selling of this show was Billy Joel. So to get the audience primed for what was to come, we spotlighted the band on stage. Then we moved the band up and back (thanks to some very expensive hydraulics) and brought the dancers onto the stage. This confused the audience. They didn't know whether to look at the band or the dancers. They felt they were missing something. At a musical, you follow the person who's singing, right? Almost all musicals begin with an overture, but you don't *see* the overture; the orchestra's in the pit, and the audience knows it's not a part of the action. In this case, how were they supposed to know that? It took a couple of numbers for the audience to understand who was who, and that's too long. A crucial connection between audience and stage had been missed. That connection is the reason people love theater in the first place. They caught up with it eventually, but we weren't making it easy for them.

For one of the few times in my life, I sat in the theater each night and paid as much attention to the audience as I did to the performers onstage. What I saw was simple and clear: They were miserable and confused after Act One, but standing and cheering at the end of Act Two. Act Two was working. Act One was not.

One night I went outside and crossed the street to the restaurant where some of the audience goes during intermission. I overheard one waiter tell a couple, "Don't worry. The second act is much better." When the waiters in town know the problem and you don't do something about it, that's denial.

It wasn't possible to make major changes before the opening night in Chicago, and the resulting reviews were not kind, to say the least. The critics praised the dancers and they loved Act Two, but they thought Act One was confusing. They used words that had never been attached to my work before, words like "mess" and "risible." The show was in trouble.

My old friend Jennifer Tipton had flown in from New York for the opening. We had breakfast the next morning with the reviews in front of us. A Broadway veteran of thirty years, she didn't try to console me. She said, "You know they're right."

I nodded my head. "Yes, I know." This was, as the clichés have it, the first step toward a solution. Denial was no longer an option.

The next day, a Monday, I had to face a cast and crew that was bruised, tired, and worried. To compound the trauma, a New York newspaper had decided to reprint one of the scathing reviews, breaking the long tradition of letting Broadway-bound shows work out their kinks out of town in private. Publishing out-of-town reviews before a single New York performance was simply not done. This set off a public debate between the theater world and the press. *Movin' Out* had become news for all the wrong reasons. People, it seemed, were gunning for us.

Changes had to be made, and I would have three weeks in Chicago and only three rehearsal days in New York to make them before the first previews prior to our Broadway opening.

I was not a novice at the art of change. I knew the repertoire of tweak and cut and add and replace and reposition. I had been doing this for years.

What made this especially challenging is that there were so many different areas to look at. Was the problem in the music? I cut one song, thought about putting in three or four others, wound up adding one. Was the problem in the narrative? I simplified the story and pushed one character forward, so that more of the show revolved around him. To do that I had to shrink another character who had functioned almost as a narrator in one incarnation, like the Stage Manager in *Our Town*. Was the problem scenic or visual? We'd had some wig problems early on that made it hard for the audience to recognize the characters from one scene to the next, but the wardrobe and scenery now seemed pretty much okay. I'd replay the entire show in my head at night and wonder, Is the wrong song playing here? Is the wrong character in this scene? Are they coming in the wrong door? Are they doing the wrong steps? Everywhere I looked, I thought, Hey, let's fix *that*.

The wonderful and scary thing about solving creative problems is that there isn't one right answer. There are a thousand possible answers, but the valuable and practical thing to do is *fix the things you know how to fix*. That's why a failure of skill is unforgivable: If you don't have a broad base of skills, you're limiting the number of problems you can solve when trouble hits.

Fortunately, I had more than just the skill to choreograph. Most of the decisions that had to be made now were *directing* and *editing* choices, and I could do that, too. During the sleepless nights in Chicago when I reran the show from memory, I looked for the changes that would bring Act One into tighter focus and let Act Two run as gloriously as it had from the start. I was tempted to believe that the scenes worked fine in their current order—just because I had seen them that way for so long now (see *repetition*, above). But I needed to resist that temptation. It was time to clean the slate and look at everything fresh.

My support came from my routine, my sustenance from my rituals of self-reliance. I made it a point of honor to be at the gym, two blocks away from my hotel room, each morning at 7:00 A.M. for a two-hour workout. I needed the routine not just for endurance, it was also important for me to believe that I was still in shape, that my body functioned. If everything fell apart and I was wiped out, I could always go back to dancing. At night after each show, with my mind still racing, I would follow the same comforting heat ritual, pouring myself into a hot bath and letting my brain go blank.

The producers, to their credit, were supportive. While I was making changes onstage, they could have made the ultimate change: fire me and bring in another director to save the show. But they didn't. They rallied around us. We were all in this together, paddling a leaky canoe in a choppy stream heading toward New York City. Our mantra was "Stay in the canoe."

When I was making all these changes, in effect I was scratching again, trying to claw out an idea that would clarify the show for the audience. To some degree, the scratching and changes worked. The show was getting better. It wasn't frozen yet, but at least it was Jell-O.

I also listened to people I trusted. One friend told me she had sat next to a woman at a performance who put her hands over her eyes for one song and then over her ears for another. My friend asked the woman at intermission, "What's going on? Don't you like it?"

"Oh no," said the woman, "I like it. I just don't know where to get my information."

This was echoed by another friend, a major director, who told me, "You're doing too much, trying too hard. Make each scene about one thing, not three things."

Making the changes was a brutal process. When you cut and replace words on your computer, the words don't have feelings; they can't talk back to you. It's the same when you work with film at an editing bay or with acrylics at an easel. Film and paint don't cry "foul." But I was dealing with human beings. When I enlarged a part or cut a role, people's noses got out of joint.

One of the most important changes was to scale back the lighting on the band; we had to make it clearer to the audience that the dancers were the story. Musicians are usually the coolest of pros, but they howled when we took the spotlights off them. Still, they understood that it was in their interest (spelled j-o-b-s) for the show to work. They accepted the change as gracefully as could be expected.

From my life in the dance world, I understood the diva mind-set of gifted performers. I was asking a huge amount from them. They had to rehearse all day to learn the material we were changing, then had to pour their hearts out at night onstage in the old show that had received those terrible notices, at least until the new version was ready to be unveiled. For every cut I made in a dancer's role I tried to make it up in another part of the show.

This was dangerous work, a high-wire act. When you make a change, it has to be a win-win change. You have to hack out something that doesn't work and replace it with something that does. I knew that I would only get one chance to make each change for the better. If I tested out a change, dismissed it, and went back to the old way, I'd start to lose the cast's trust. *Hadn't that come out because it wasn't working? What makes it any better now?* I didn't need the perfect solution to every problem, but I did need a workable solution—a lot of them.

Even after we had cut secondary characters, taken out several songs, and centered the show's conflicts on just a few characters, the audience was still confused. At this point, bless their coal-black little hearts, the critics turned out to be enormously useful. My son, Jesse, back in New York, did a marvelous thing. He knew I couldn't stomach reading the reviews too closely, so he read them all and took out the venom, concentrating on the substance of the critiques. He charted their comments, and when we found more than two critics citing the same problem we said, "Okay, this is a hot zone."

The one thing all the critics agreed on was that the show lacked an effective opening number. The time had come to tackle that problem at last.

Once you climb out of denial, it's easy to see what you need to do. I had been so hell-bent on breaking the status quo and flouting convention with *Movin' Out* that I had failed to see how convention might be my salvation. Going back and reviewing the opening numbers for dozens of successful musicals (scratch in the best places), I found that many of them used the ancient device of a prologue to introduce the characters. That would be our answer: a prologue. At this point, a new muse, Serendipity, dropped into our lives. Actually, she came first to Santo Loquasto, my production designer. Santo was in a supermarket when Billy Joel's song "It's Still Rock and Roll to Me" came over the store's sound system. As he walked the aisles of the store, Santo noticed that the 4/4 beat of the song perfectly matched the rhythm of the opening to a twenty-year-old dance of mine called *Ocean's Motion,* which was set to Chuck Berry songs. It takes an extraordinarily perceptive colleague to pick up on a similarity like this; this was not the first time I was thrilled to have Santo on my side. I checked it out, and Billy's song and the old steps fit together beautifully, and even better, it had roles for five principals, just what we needed. I pulled out a tape of *Ocean's Motion,* taught the steps to the cast, and—voilà!—we had a new opening number for all twenty-four dancers, taught and staged in one three-hour session. We finally had an opening that let the audience shake hands with the dancers.

We still had the problem of setting the audience's expectations before they walked in the door. That word *musical* was in the way. But what else could we call it? The audience was loving what we were doing now, it was blowing them away, and maybe we don't want to call it dance, but what else is it?

It was Billy who broke the logjam on this issue. "Why not just call it its title?" he asked. "Then we won't have to call it anything."

And so *Movin' Out, The New Broadway Musical* became, simply, *Movin' Out.*

And in the end, it was all worth the effort. The audience, which had loved Act Two all along, was no longer confused by the beginning. The reviews in New York were much more fun to read than the ones in Chicago had been.

In the end, grueling as it was, my fast turn with failure was an empowering experience. When *Movin' Out* "failed" in Chicago, I had two ways to respond: (a) stay in denial, bring the show "as is" to New York, and take my chances that the New York critics would miss the flaws that the Chicago reviewers so obviously picked up; or (b) dig in and fix things, see the out-of-town reviews as a blessing, a reprieve, a miracle shot at getting a second chance.

Obviously, I took the latter course. But the same goes for you. Failing, and learning from it, is necessary. Until you've done it, you're missing an important piece of your creative arsenal.

exercises

31 Give Yourself a Second Chance

No matter who you are, at some point you will present your work to the world—and the world will find it wanting. Patrons shrug. Critics hiss. Audiences stay away in droves. Even loyal friends avert their eyes.

Incredibly, there is good news here. Sometimes you will fail, but the world will give you a second chance to get it right.

This happens every day in the film business. A film director gets to shoot a scene over and over again until he is satisfied. If he's still not satisfied the next day, he can rewrite the scene and shoot it again. If an actor isn't working out, the director hires someone else. Later on, he gets a few more second chances in postproduction. He can cover up his sins by editing and re-editing. He can alter the entire mood of a film by replacing the music score. He gets yet another chance when the finished cut is shown to preview audiences. With so much money on the line, film people like to test the market—and sometimes the director will accept the audiences' comments and make more changes. In many ways a director's job is how he uses all his second chances.

When I worked with Milos Forman on *Amadeus* in 1980, I noted a distinct change in his work habits and attitude in the three years since we had worked together on *Hair. Hair* had not been a happy experience for Milos. He was tormented by his producers during filming, even though he was fresh off the critical and commercial success of *One Flew Over the Cuckoo's Nest,* which had swept all five major Academy Awards. The *Hair* experience ran so counter to Milos's sense of artistry and control that he would sometimes "nap" for sixteen hours rather than face the bullying producers. *Hair* did some business (as they say) but it was not the success we all were hoping for.

Milos applied everything he'd learned about power and control on the set of *Hair* to *Amadeus.* On *Amadeus,* he was not only the director, he was also a producer. If it failed, at least he would have the certainty that it was *his* failure, accomplished without compro-

227

mises. He stacked everything in his favor: He made sure he had a great story in Peter Shaffer's original play, which had succeeded with audiences around the world. He had sublime music, all Mozart, to work with. He had great locations in Prague. Many of the actors, from both sides of the Atlantic, were either friends or people who had worked with him before. There were no star egos to deal with. Milos was taking no chances—and the results speak for themselves.

Not every art form offers such comfort, or tosses you a life jacket. A sculptor whose work is deemed a failure cannot go back and rework the metal, clay, or stone. He must absorb the criticism and do better the next time. It's pretty much the same for painters and photographers. You don't get do-overs in the plastic arts.

It's the same in the dance world: No do-overs. You mount your ballet, the audience applauds or yawns, which determines whether the work gets mounted again. A hit can be revived season after season. A flop is forgotten within a week.

Wouldn't it be nice if we could predict and preempt a work's less-than-favorable reception, if we could give ourselves a second chance before we find out we really need it?

Well, actually we often can. Before I sent this manuscript to my publisher, I showed it to twelve trusted friends, and factored their comments into the text. Where more than one of them was confused by a section of text, I reworked it to make it clearer. By building failure, or at least the prospect of failure, into the process, I gave myself a second chance.

By acknowledging failure, you take the first step to conquering it.

32 Build Your Own Validation Squad

We all seek approval and validation for our efforts. In the beginning we desperately seek the approval of others—of *anybody*—to assure us that we're on the right path, that we aren't wasting our time, that we haven't made a monumental error. But that neediness fades as we get older and more confident. We become a better and clearer judge of our own work. If a piece is good, we know it before the public applauds and the reviews come in. If it's bad, we know that, too. As Montaigne said, "We easily confess to others an advantage of courage, strength, experience, activity, and beauty. But an advantage in judgment we yield to none."

Don't misunderstand. I'm not saying that it is all right to be a self-contained, solipsistic, don't-give-a-damn-what-anyone-thinks egotist operating under the credo of "As long as I like it, it's good." That way lies madness, or at least embarrassing self-indulgence. But there comes a time when you have no choice but to trust your judgment above all others'. As Billy Wilder once said, "If I like something, I am lucky enough, fool enough, or smart enough to believe that other people are going to like it too." Circular logic? Yes. But at least *you* are drawing the circle.

As we mature, we need to build criticism into the working process, as we do with failure. For a long time now I've had my own validation squad, a small group of people I invite to see my works in progress. I trust them to look at my crudest, clumsiest noodlings and reward me with their candor. I put a lot of faith in what they say. My criteria for these validators are very basic: I pick people who (a) have talents I admire greatly (so I know they have judgment), (b) happen to be my friends (so I know they have my best interests at heart), (c) don't feel they are competing with me (so I know they have no agenda no matter what they say), and (d) have hammered my work in the past (so I know they are capable of brutal honesty). I don't want my feelings spared; I want an honest answer to the eternal question "Do we care?" If you choose your validators, you never have to look at them and wonder "Who died and made you God?" Because you did.

Look around you. Who are the brightest, most talented people you know? Choose them, "qualify" them (in the same way that a salesperson "qualifies" customers by determining if they have the money to buy, a need for the product, and the authority to make the buying decision), and then get them involved. All you need are people with good judgment in other parts of their lives who care about you and will give you their honest opinion with no strings attached. The last point is crucial: All things being equal, the validation that matters most is the kind that comes with no agenda.

Chapter 12

the long run

I was fifty-eight years old when I finally felt like a "master choreographer." The occasion was my 128th ballet, *The Brahms-Haydn Variations*, created for American Ballet Theatre (see page 132). For the first time in my career I felt in control of all the components that go into making a dance—the music, the steps, the patterns, the deployment of people onstage, the clarity of purpose. Finally I had the skills to close the gap between what I could see in my mind and what I could actually get onto the stage.

Why did it take 128 pieces before I felt this way? A better question would be, Why not? What's wrong with getting better as you get more work under your belt? The libraries and archives and museums are packed with early bloomers and one-trick ponies who said everything they had to say in their first novel, who could only compose one good tune, whose canvases kept repeating the same dogged theme. My respect has always gone to those who are in it for the long haul. When people who have demonstrated talent fizzle out or disappear after early creative success, it's not because their gifts, that famous "one percent inspiration," abandoned them; more likely they abandoned their gift through a failure of perspiration.

The Italian physicist Cesare Marchetti set out to define the patterns of our creative lives. Marchetti totaled up the cumulative production of creative works by more than a hundred recognized geniuses and found in it an S-shaped curve that mimics the growth curve of all natural life. The curve is flat when there is no productivity; it gets steeper as productivity increases. He charted everyone from Botticelli to Bach to Shakespeare to Einstein to Brahms, comparing their output against their progressing age. He found that, on average, creative production is limited in our youth (when we are learning), hits full stride in our prime middle years, and trails off in our later years when we become exhausted of ideas, energy, and motivation. Here's his chart for Mozart:

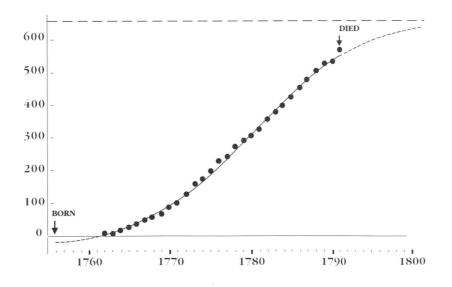

Mozart's an intriguing example because he wrote a lot of music (626 compositions by most counts), and it's all been cataloged, as if expressly for chartmakers like Marchetti, by Ludwig Köchel—from Mozart's earliest symphony, listed as K. 1, to his final D minor Requiem, K. 626. (Köchel listed forty or so minor compositions that may be works of other composers, but his is the universally accepted catalog of Mozart's output. Not everyone cares: Professional musicians generally refer to Mozart's delightful A major piano concerto as "the A major," concertgoers know it as his twenty-third, while only the serious librarians among us call it K. 488. Film buffs may recall it as the Köchel listing a dying Ali MacGraw struggled to remember in her hospital bed in *Love Story*.)

The only problem: Mozart died young, at age thirty-five. His chart is impressive, but it feels unfinished, cut short. Who's to say how long and how far he would have continued. Although there are some who feel Mozart was tapped out when he died, I am not one of them. I think he was on the verge of a major church appointment that would have provided him with the resources and opportunity to create great liturgical music, but we'll never know.

The other problem with this type of analysis is that it turns everyone into a statistic. Applying algorithms to creativity is like biochemists trying to formulate the chemistry of love. It takes some of the romance out of the enterprise. The best that can be said of a chart like this is that it measures *devotion to craft*. The chart tells you nothing about quality, about whether Mozart's last piece is an improvement on the first, or whether the two are linked. It charts activity and persistence, not artistic growth.

But let's not knock devotion to craft. There is no long run without devotion, commitment, persistence.

My heroes are the artists whose bodies of work are consistently surprising, consistently fresh: Mozart, Beethoven, Verdi, Dostoyevsky, Yeats, Cézanne, Kurosawa, Balanchine. They all had stunning early triumphs, and they kept getting better through their middle and later years.

The Dostoyevsky who wrote *The House of the Dead* in 1860 is the same writer who wrote *Crime and Punishment* in his middle years and *The Brothers Karamazov* in his later years. But he is a vastly different and more profound writer in his later years. He continued to grow.

The pattern is even more obvious with Beethoven, whose musical output divides neatly into early, middle, and late periods, each with a distinct style, each representing an advancement of the form. No one who studies his thirty-two piano sonatas or his sixteen string quartets can miss this.

It's equally obvious with Verdi, who had more than his share of masterworks before surprising the world with the ineffable *Falstaff* at age eighty-one. That he was still growing in his ninth decade makes the arc of Verdi's creative output in his early, middle, and late periods stand out in sharper relief. When a man turns out a masterpiece long after his peers and rivals have died, you see anew everything that came before: the continuity, the progression in the arc. The same can be said of Cézanne or Matisse or Yeats. Their later work astonishes profoundly and means more because of how it shows their development from their earlier efforts.

These are giants and masters. You surely have your own pantheon of heroes who learned and grew as they pursued their chosen paths. Regardless of how poorly we compare to their talent and quality, we can still emulate them; they prove that there's no reason our creativity must dry up as we age.

True, for some the will and desire fade because they have enough money or are facing poor health or feel they've said it all. (I think here of Rossini bursting onto the scene at age twenty-four with *The Barber of Seville*, then abandoning opera thirteen years later after the hysterical acclaim for his *William Tell*; he lived another thirty-nine years and wrote piano pieces and songs, but not another opera. Or Arthur Rimbaud, the French symbolist poet who stopped writing before age twenty, just halfway into the course of his life.)

Some people find their curiosity shutting down as they age, losing their taste for the new and settling in to reread their favorite books and listen to the music of their youth. And it's certainly possible to get distracted by family obligations.

But there's nothing necessary or inevitable about it. We can fight the lockdown of our curiosity. We can sign up for the long run even if we might not cover the course as elegantly as our heroes.

As we age, it's hard to recapture the recklessness of youth, when new ideas flew off us like light from a pinwheel sparkler. But we more than compensate for this with the ideas we do generate, and with our hard-earned wisdom about how to capture and, more importantly, *connect* those ideas. When I was young I understood very little about the value of a spine to a piece; I wasted time and energy by moving blindly in many directions, when a clearer understanding of spine would have kept me on the path I wanted. I've learned so much more about my own preferences. I know that my best work comes out of my creative DNA that seeks to reconcile the competing forces of *zoe* and *bios*. I've grown more efficient in my efforts; I've seen enough dead ends to know when an enticing trail will get me nowhere. And I've learned to see continuity in all I do.

The dance critic Arlene Croce said to me, "The curtain goes up once on your dance and comes down once." She meant that what I do is all of a piece, that no matter how many individual dances I create, each will be one more movement in a very long dance.

If you want to hear this kind of continuity in its clearest developmental form, listen to the Beatles in chronological order. No one was more popular, more universally admired, more commercially successful—and no other group was reinventing itself so consistently yet identifiably. From the sunny optimism of "I Want to Hold Your Hand" to the sagging resignation of "Let It Be" you get a complete creative arc of 13 albums and 163 songs recorded in eight whirlwind years from 1963 to 1971. Each collection is complete yet foreshadows the songs to come. *Beatles 65* suggests *Rubber Soul* which suggests *Revolver* which foreshadows *Sgt. Pepper's Lonely Hearts Club Band* and *Magical Mystery Tour* and *The White Album* and *Abbey Road.* The Beatles ended when they had to end, and they never got back together, which would have muddied the waters. Their music is the most easily discernible creative arc of my lifetime.

If you find, in your own work, that ideas you didn't have room for at a particular time nonetheless lingered and arose later, you are coming close to an ideal creative state, one where creativity becomes a self-perpetuating habit. You are linking your art. Everything in your life feeds into your work, and the work feeds into more work.

Happily, this ideal creative state is not a random event, not a stroke of luck or coincidence. It is within your grasp. You can construct it and control it.

When I look back on my best work, it was inevitably created in what I call **The Bubble.** I eliminated every distraction, sacrificed almost everything that gave me pleasure, placed myself in a single-minded isolation chamber, and structured my life so that everything was not only feeding the work but subordinated to it. It is not a particularly sociable way to operate. It's actively anti-social. On the other hand, it is pro-creative.

I used to think I was alone in the extremity of my views until I read David Remnick's admiring *New Yorker* profile of Philip Roth in May 2000. Roth, sixty-eight years old at the time, was a model of late-life rejuvenation, having produced in his sixties four remarkable novels in a row: *American Pastoral, I Married a Communist, Sabbath's Theater,* and *The Human Stain.* The story explored how and why this happened.

Roth immerses himself in a creative bubble. He lives alone in the country. He works seven days a week, waking early and walking to a two-room studio fifty yards from his house. He stays in the studio all day, writes Remnick, and into the evening:

Nothing gets in. In the late afternoons, he takes long walks, often trying to figure out connections and solve problems in the novel that's possessing him.

"I live alone, there's no one else to be responsible for or to, or to spend time with," Roth said. "My schedule is absolutely my own. Usually, I write all day, but if I want to go back to the studio in the evening after dinner, I don't have to sit in the living room because someone else has been alone all day. I

don't have to sit there and be entertaining or amusing. I go back out and I work for two or three more hours. If I wake up at two in the morning—this happens rarely, but it sometimes happens—and something has dawned on me, I turn the light on and I write in the bedroom. I have these little yellow things all over the place. I read till all hours if I want to. If I get up at five and I can't sleep and I want to work, I go out and I go to work. So I work, I'm on call. I'm like a doctor and it's an emergency. And I'm the emergency.

Roth had pared his life down to the minimum number of moving parts. Near his desk he kept two small signs, one reading "Stay Put," the other "No Optional Striving"—reminders to avoid the temptation of anything other than the five essentials: food, writing, exercise, sleep, and solitude.

It might sound like a grim, deprived life, except for the fact that Roth was happy and in a state of fulfilled glory. His unilateral mission, which he likened to the hunkering down of a soldier with a barracks life, put his craft and imagination on permanent duty:

"It's a wonderful experience," Roth said. "That act of passionate and minute memory is what binds your days together—days, weeks, months—and living with that is my greatest pleasure. I think for any novelist it has to be the greatest pleasure, that's why you're doing it—to make the daily connections. I do it by living a very austere life."

To me, Roth's bubble didn't sound grim or misguided or misanthropic. He had ideas that needed expressing. A monastic life was his recipe for handling those ideas.

Being in the bubble does not have to mean exiling yourself from people and the world. It is more a state of mind, a willingness to subtract anything that disconnects you from your work. It doesn't have to be antisocial. Richard Avedon has lived in his own kind of bubble for much of his creative life. His bubble happens to be a large studio on Manhattan's Upper East Side, swarming with assistants. Avedon himself is a singularly social creature—very outgoing, caring, and observant of other people, devoted to close friends, and blessed with great social skills. It is quite probable that, with the exception of heads of state and talk-show hosts, he has met more notable people than anyone on earth. And yet Avedon's studio has all the elements of the bubble ideal. It is cloistered, self-contained, and free of distractions, allowing him to work in populated solitude. His secret: He has the camera and the charisma to lure the world into his bubble. And in that bubble, familiar to him yet open to unfamiliar visitations, he prepares, he remembers, he focuses, he connects, and he refines and grows his art.

There are no rules. Bubbles can exist amid chaos. They can be mobile: There's nothing more hectic than a rock band on tour, but the confining schedule of planes, limos, hotels, backstage, and onstage becomes a bubble of sorts over the course of several months—and a touring songwriter, cut off from home, will often come back with a pile of new songs for the next disk. It wasn't intentional; the bubble made him do it.

I realize that not all of us have the resources to achieve the pure bubble state of self-sustaining artists like Roth and Avedon. We have families, jobs, and responsibilities that impinge on our desire to create. I hesitate to make the long run a gauntlet of all or nothing that forces us to go to monastic and hard-hearted extremes. At its worst, the bubble conjures up images of the artist toiling away in his studio, ignoring the cries of his children and the sacrifices his wife is making so he can concentrate on his creations. I don't find that a heroic image; I much prefer the thought of J. S. Bach, a loving family man and teacher who managed to create masterpieces in every existing musical form known in his time. And when they didn't exist, he invented them. But even within our distracted existence, we have to cultivate a version of a bubble if we want to work freely and with maximum fluency in making connections and harnessing our memory—and to maintain all this as a habit. The bubble gives you that chance. It is the ideal state where nothing is wasted, where every detail feeds your art because it has nowhere else to go.

The birds sing and you hear a tune.

The sunlight falls on the studio wall and you see a new color or pattern.

A group of people standing across the street reveals a new geometry for arranging actors onstage.

An overheard snatch of conversation inspires a line of dialogue for your script.

A photo in the newspaper suggests a new dramatic situation, and you rush to the desk to get it down on paper.

This is the bubble. Everything you see, hear, touch, and smell gets trapped within immediately. As you pursue your art over the years, accumulating skills and experiences, you respect this precious ideal state more deeply. This is why writers go off to secluded colonies, and artists work in studios away from their homes, and composers write in soundproof chambers, and academics require sabbaticals (although some would say they already live in ivory-tower bubbles). Being in the bubble does not mean being a hermit. You can function out in the world (indeed, you have to), but wherever you go the bubble goes with you. You know the cost of distractions, yet you recognize the need for balance if you are to maintain the relationships that sustain your creativity. Sooner or later, you're going to have to come out of the bubble, and it would be nice if there were loved ones to greet you when you do.

When creativity has become your habit; when you've learned to manage time, resources, expectations, and the demands of others; when you understand the value and place of validation, continuity, and purity of purpose—then you're on the way to an artist's ultimate goal: the achievement of mastery.

The Shakers, the nineteenth-century religious community of self-sufficient craftsmen, made furniture and weavings and tools that were truly masterful. Yet they recognized that there was a fine line between mastery and arrogance; they did not want anyone to think of himself as a master, because there is only One Master. They constructed a system to keep themselves constantly inexperienced. When members of the community mastered a craft (whether it was carpentry or making brooms), the elders would switch them to another task, putting them out in the fields or in the blacksmith shop, where they'd have to start all over again. I admire their devotion to the challenge of the new, though I question their fear of mastery itself. In my experience, every time you set out to create something new, you have to prove to yourself you can still do it at least as well as, if not better than, you did it before. You can not rest on your creative laurels.

Mastery is an elusive concept. You never know when you achieve it absolutely—and it may not help you to feel you've attained it. (Alexander the Great wept when he had no more worlds to conquer.) We can recognize it more readily in others than we can in ourselves. We all have to discover our own definition of it. I take mine from the story of "Giotto's O." The fourteenth-century Italian artist, when asked to supply proof of his artistic skill for Pope Benedict XI, complied by drawing a perfect circle with a single fluent movement. Giotto was playing on an established topos, or convention, in art theory that linked consummate artistic skill with the ability to draw a circle freehand.

I was reminded of that topos when I was on tour in The Hague and went to an exhibition of Rembrandt self-portraits. An early painting, *The Painter in His*

Studio, caught my eye. It shows Rembrandt cloaked in shadow gazing intently at an easel that dominates the foreground. As I turned the corner to another room, I was stunned by a work made forty years later, *Self Portrait with Two Circles.* The jump in technique between the two portraits is phenomenal. The first reveals a painter who is tentative and unsure of his beginning. You see it in the flat, lifeless brush strokes. The second shows a painter drenched in confidence. The brush strokes are thick, three-dimensional, centuries ahead of their time. They could easily be the strokes of a nineteenth-century master.

But far more striking than the development of technique was how Rembrandt portrayed his personal growth. In the first, he is small, intimidated, facing a giant canvas that he can hardly bring himself to touch. We all know that feeling when we're starting out. In the second, he is engaging us directly, dominating the foreground, with two half circles behind him. Here was an artist's growth made tangible. I remembered Giotto's topos and how the closed form of the circle symbolized eternity and perfection through its association with the halos of the saints. How wise of Rembrandt, I thought, and how human to install himself between the two half circles, as if he existed between youthful and mature mastery, between painting as he found it and as he would leave it.

I suspect all of us have our own topos, our own sense of what mastery means and how close we come to achieving it. If to an artist it means drawing a perfect circle, then to a musician it might be writing reams of variations and fugues and complex counterpoint from a single simple theme. To a storyteller it might be the ability to weave a complete story on the spot from someone else's opening line. To a chef it's creating an exquisite meal with whatever ingredients are at hand. To a designer, it's making a fashion statement out of any snatch of fabric. To me, it's creating a dance with an impossible timetable, constricted rehearsals, and restricted access to dancers. When you can create beauty and wonder from the metaphorical stone that the builder refused, you have achieved mastery.

More than anything, I associate mastery with optimism. It's the feeling at the start of a project when I believe that my whole career has been preparation for this moment and I am saying, "Okay, let's begin. Now I am ready." Of course, you're never one hundred percent ready, but that's a part of mastery, too: It masks the insecurities and the gaps in technique and lets you believe you are capable of anything.

When it all comes together, a creative life has the nourishing power we normally associate with food, love, and faith. On Saturday, September 8, 2001, my company gave a free performance for two thousand people in the plaza that separated the twin towers of New York's World Trade Center. We were the last people to perform there. Three days later, the day of the attacks, I was putting the finishing touches on a theatrical project to which I had devoted most of my year, preparing for a rehearsal in the late morning at a studio in midtown Manhattan. As the chaos of 9/11 developed, I thought about working with my dancers that day, but decided it was impossible, for so many reasons. I phoned all the dancers to check on their welfare, and I told them there was no obligation to attend rehearsal the next day. Yet they all showed up, ready for work, arriving in a shaken Manhattan, with its bridges and tunnels only just reopened, from Brooklyn, Staten Island, New Jersey, and Westchester County to the north.

We could have easily become absorbed by the tragedy, lost in it and paralyzed by it, but what came back to us was the instinct to dance. I began as a dancer, and in those days of pain and shock I went back to where I started. Creating dance is the thing I know best. It is how I recognize myself. Even in the worst of times, such habits sustain, protect, and, in the most unlikely way, lift us up. I cannot think of a more compelling reason to foster the creative habit.

It permits me to walk into a white room . . . and walk out dancing.

ACKNOWLEDGMENTS

My agent, Mark Reiter, may he live forever.

My trainer, Sean Kelleher, the only person who can make me do
what I don't want to do.

My teammates at Simon & Schuster: Jeff Neuman, David Rosenthal,
Ruth Fecych, Jon Malki, Jackie Seow, Linda Dingler, Elizabeth Hayes,
and Julian Peploe, for midwifing this book to life.

My validation squad: Richard Avedon, Robert and Eric Batscha, Lewis Cole,
Robert Gottlieb, John Halpern, Ellen Jacobs, Bredo Johnsen, Susan Kagan,
Irving Lavin, Santo Loquasto, Larry Moss, Mike Nichols, Jed Perl,
Maurice Sendak, Norma Stevens, Patsy Tarr, Jennifer Tipton.

Nancy Gabriel of IMG Artists, for getting the ball rolling; Meg Kowalski and
Karen Brown, for their help pushing it along
and

Four generations of dancers.

ABOUT THE AUTHOR

Twyla Tharp, one of America's greatest choreographers, began her career in 1965, and in the ensuing years has created more than 130 dances for her company as well as for the Joffrey Ballet, the New York City Ballet, Paris Opera Ballet, London's Royal Ballet, and American Ballet Theatre. Working to the music of everyone from Bach, Beethoven, and Mozart to Jelly Roll Morton, Frank Sinatra, and Bruce Springsteen, she is a pioneer in melding modern dance and ballet with popular music. In film, she collaborated with Milos Forman on *Hair, Ragtime,* and *Amadeus.* For television, she directed *Baryshnikov by Tharp,* which won two Emmy awards. For the Broadway stage, she directed the theatrical version of *Singin' in the Rain,* and in 2003 won a Tony Award for *Movin' Out,* which she conceived, directed, and choreographed to the songs of Billy Joel. She is the recipient of a MacArthur Fellowship. In 1993, she was inducted into the American Academy of Arts & Sciences, and in 1997 was made an honorary member of the American Academy of Arts and Letters. She has received eighteen honorary doctorates. She lives and works in New York City.

Mark Reiter has collaborated on eleven previous books. He is also a literary agent in Bronxville, New York.